MELODY BARKER

While
You Are
Waiting

How to Make the Most of Where You Are

Everything is Possible!

While You Are Waiting
How to Make the Most of Where You Are

Author Photo: Tiffany King | Makeup Artist: Bethany Joy Chamberlin

Cover Design & Interior Layout: www.palmtreeproductions.com

Printed in the USA

ISBN (print): 978-0-9975585-0-0

ISBN (Kindle): 978-0-9975585-1-7

Library of Congress Control Number: 2016906869

Scripture references:

Scripture taken from the HOLY BIBLE, NEW INTERNATIONAL VERSION * is marked NIV. Copyright © 1973, 1978, 1984 Biblica. Used by permission of Zondervan. All rights reserved.

Scripture taken from The Message * is marked MSG. Copyright © 1993, 1994, 1995, 1996, 2000, 2001, 2002. Used by permission of NavPress Publishing Group. Colorado Springs, CO. All rights reserved.

Scripture taken from Holy Bible, New Living Translation is marked NLT. Copyright © 1996, 2004, 2015 by Tyndale House Foundation. Used by permission of Tyndale House Publishers Inc., Carol Stream, Illinois 60188. All rights reserved.

Scripture taken from the New King James Version of the Bible is marked NKJV. Copyright © 1982 by Thomas Nelson, Inc. Used by permission. All rights reserved.

To Contact the Author:

www.melodybarker.com

Table of Contents

A Note From the Author

I desire readers will find hope, encouragement and direction to develop and enjoy their lives to the fullest. I have shared some of my toughest moments, heartache, compassion, and the need for forgiveness. I pray that God will bring healing to the hearts of those who read it and that they will give their hopes and dreams the action that faith requires. Thank you for taking time to read this.

- Melody Barker

Dedication

For My Grandparents:
Charles & Frances Hunter
and Clint & Wilma Barker

Thank you for the generational blessing and heritage that you started when you chose to follow Jesus. I honor you and I thank you for the gift of legacy that you gave me.

Charles & Frances Hunter
Maternal Grandparents

Clint & Wilma Barker
Paternal Grandparents

Acknowledgments

To My Parents:
Robert Barker and Joan Hunter

Thank you for all of the sacrifices you made in order to shape and mold my life and character. Thank you for your unconditional love and instilling in me that I can do anything and I do not have to take a back seat to anyone.

Robert Barker
Father

Joan Hunter
Mother

To My Friend:
Tiffany

Thank you for your friendship, support and help. Thank you for all of the laundry, dishes, and puppy care you did during the writing of this book. Thank you for believing in me and the message I want to share, even when I doubted myself. I am so thankful that we have been friends for so many years. I thank God that we have witnessed the goodness of God and His hand of protection on our lives and the pursuit of living a great life. Thank  you for your help in writing and editing this book, but most of all, thank you for being my best friend.

Praise for While You Are Waiting

"So many people waiting ... and waiting ... watching the clock ... and waiting some more ... never really enjoying the journey or appreciating "the process" because they are always focused on the "waiting." Melody hits a homerun with her new book, *While You Are Waiting*, helping to shift our vision clearly into focus and redirecting our hearts heavenward. Her life experiences and personal testimonies will encourage you, inspire you and anoint you with fresh oil. We love Melody and her heart of ministry towards others, we love this book and we know you will too!"

Joshua & Janet Angela Mills
Bestselling Authors & Evangelists
New Wine International, Inc.
Palm Springs, California / London, Canada

"Patience is a virtue, but not one popular in today's culture. *While You Are Waiting* presents wonderful keys for actively waiting well. Concerning marriage, our friend Melody Barker proposes not pushing the pause button on life, and recommends always being the real you in all relationships. We fully agree. Melody practices what she preaches. We celebrate that she is a whole person, loving and embracing life, even as she waits for her prince to come and sweep her off her feet. Regardless of what you are waiting for, following Melody's advice will help you to wait expectantly and proactively—to wait well."

Dr. Dan and Linda Wilson
Authors of *Lovemaking* and *7 Secrets of a Supernatural Marriage*
Supernatural Marriage and Missions

"For many years I have read many incredible writings by Melody. This book is by far the best she has ever done. This has not been an easy book to live out, but what the waiting has done for her and how she has walked out these opportunities will challenge you to do the same.

She has shared her heart, mainly so you don't feel you are the only one going through this time of waiting. Allow her to lead you through this time in your life and grow through this, instead of whining and complaining.

Everyone needs to read this book. It puts a whole new perspective on waiting. It will teach you how to wait well. Enjoy!"

Joan Hunter
Author, Evangelist, Proud Mother
Joan Hunter Ministries

"*While You are Waiting*, why not write a book and share the secrets of waiting well with others? Some authors write from memories—after they are on the other side of their journey, but Melody shares her unfolding experience with you <u>while she is still in her waiting season</u>. Powerful. Beautiful. Honest. Real."

Wendy K. Walters
Motivational Speaker, Master Coach
wendykwalters.com

While *You Are* Waiting

Introduction

You can get so confused that you'll start in to race down long wiggled roads at a break-necking pace and grind on for miles across weirdish wild space, headed, I fear, toward a most useless place. The Waiting Place ... for people just waiting. Waiting for a train to go or a bus to come, or a plane to go or the mail to come, or the rain to go or the phone to ring, or the snow to snow or waiting around for a Yes or a No or waiting for their hair to grow. Everyone is just waiting. Waiting for the fish to bite or waiting for wind to fly a kite or waiting around for Friday night or waiting, perhaps, for their Uncle Jake or a pot to boil, or a Better Break or a string of pearls, or a pair of pants or a wig with curls, or Another Chance. Everyone is just waiting.

—Dr. Seuss
Excerpt From *Oh the Places You Will Go*

Everyone is waiting for something. Waiting is a common thread that weaves through the life of every human being. How we wait and what we are doing while we wait can become something that defines us. Throughout this book and through every page, we will cover different aspects of waiting and how we can grow or change through the process. Everyone gets to experience the waiting room, but not everyone uses their time for character development. Here is something to consider: instead of saying, "this is testing my patience," say, "this is an opportunity to develop my character." A test is not something anyone looks forward to; character development is a positive message to your heart, mind and will. Choose to develop your character instead of trying to pass a test.

Through waiting and discovering the art of waiting well, I believe that my faith, character, wisdom and leadership have had the greatest growth opportunity. This is what I hope for you. I hope for you to see the potential growth that can happen in waiting well and develop perseverance to attain your heart's desire.

Somewhere around middle school, I started thinking about becoming a missionary and getting married. I think this is when most people start asking a lot of questions about "when you grow up". After discovering how much I liked living in the United States, my desire to become a full-time missionary changed. As I continued to grow up, I went on short-term mission trips and I continue to serve through missions as God speaks to me. I have also helped friends raise support for their missions, because I am passionate about helping others achieve their heart's desire. What I wanted to do with my life has changed several times, but my desire to be married has not changed. It has stayed consistent.

When I entered high school, I knew one of the things I wanted to do with my life was to be a teacher. After graduation, I had planned to go to Oral Roberts University in Tulsa, Oklahoma and pursue a teaching degree. My plans drastically had to change halfway through my senior year. The same time I received my acceptance letter I also got the news of my parents' divorce. Graduating and going to an out-of-state private college was no longer an option. Knowing what options I had in front of me, I registered at a local community college and took the first step toward my degree. In my heart, I wasn't happy. **I wasn't living the dream or the plans I had made for my life.** With each class, I became more disinterested in teaching and investigated what else my heart had to say about my future.

I was two years into college when I realized I was ignoring what I wanted to do with my life. I finished the semester and got a trade school degree in massage therapy. I was always good at massaging shoulders and I was interested in learning more about this type of therapy before I graduated high school. Massage therapy was something I wanted to do but when I shared that with those closest to me, they often showed or voiced their opinion of disappointment. Comments like, "I think you should aim higher with your life," or "I don't think that is what God has for your life" were discouraging and insulting. **Instead of pursuing what I wanted to do, I detoured and did what other people thought I should do.**

Becoming a licensed massage therapist was something I wanted to do and for a few years I let people talk me out of it. I waited to pursue the career path I wanted in order to make other people happy. I knew in my heart I still wanted to do massage therapy. Once I started school, it was difficult for me to remain confident when people made comments that I should have chosen a different direction for my life. If this sounds familiar, right now would be a good time to ask yourself:

- ❧ What part of my life am I waiting to live because other people have been able to talk me out of it?

- ❧ Do I want to stop waiting and go for it?

- ❧ Have I listened and waited long enough to the opinions of others versus listening to the desires of my heart?

- ❧ Am I ready to do something different?

Every time I made a choice, whether to change schools or to change jobs, to move or to stay, I considered the desires of my heart and what I wanted to accomplish. I also prayed and believed God to lead and guide my life, knowing that the desires of my heart were in agreement with His plans too.

When I was in my twenties, I thought about moving to Nashville, Tennessee from Dallas, Texas. My oldest sister was already living there with her husband and I thought about the possibilities that could be ahead of me if I moved. I considered staying in Dallas because I loved my church and my friends, but I felt drawn to move. After much prayer and consideration, I made plans to move. All the while, praying and believing God for His plans and purpose to be fulfilled in my life.

I lived and loved life in Nashville. I found an amazing church, made new relationships and continued to grow in my relationship with God. Four years into living in Nashville, I started traveling and helping my mom with her ministry. I was able to live in a city that I really loved and had the advantage of traveling to several countries. I found it to be the best of both worlds; living in Nashville and traveling in ministry.

In the process of traveling and always returning home, I started to feel like there was more out there than what I was doing. I recognized the abilities and gifts that God had placed inside of me and I wanted to do more with what He had given me. After six years in Nashville, I moved back to Texas, to travel and be in ministry full time. **From there, my expectations to see God do more and move more grew higher and higher.**

Every opportunity, every open door, every ministry location, I believed that God was going to use for His glory and for my heart's desire to be fulfilled. In faith, I made plans for my future, plans that would include my husband and my family. Some of the desires of my heart have changed; some have been released and some have been fulfilled. Every heart's desire is in you for a reason and the pursuit of those desires can make life exciting!

Some of the desires of my heart have changed; some have been released and some have been fulfilled.

I know that God's timing is not the same as mine. I believe the pursuit of your heart's desires can be difficult if you do not know how to wait well. This is why I believe He would have me share with you my thoughts to help you wait well and believe everything is possible.

As time has moved forward, I have seen and experienced the development and growth that my life needed and I have seen the hand of God guiding and directing my life. I do not doubt His goodness or faithfulness and I hope this will be something you start to see in your relationship with Him as well. As my heart's desires have changed or adapted I have continued to pursue God and His will for my life.

Accepting the pursuit of God's plan for your life does not mean that you can sit back and wait for everything to happen with no efforts on your own. Making a plan for your life or setting goals for achievement is a great thing to do. It is through our plans in agreement with pursuing God that He reveals His greatest glory. When we choose to look for His hand or His glory in every aspect of our life, we will find it. It is in the process of waiting that we should learn to wait well and with positive attitudes so that when the waiting time is over or the prayer is answered, we can look back and say that we waited well.

I want to share with you some of my strongest and weakest moments in order to encourage you to wait well. In my decision to wait well, I know what I am committing to, but I want to invite you to decide how you will wait from this moment on. It is an easy decision to make, but it is a choice that will need to be chosen over and over again. Daily management of this decision will cause growth and opportunities to present themselves that previously would not have been available.

Decide how you will wait from this moment on.

At the beginning of this I wrote these words: I believe that my faith, character, wisdom and leadership have had the greatest growth opportunity. I would like to share these experiences with you throughout the next few chapters of this book as well as give you hope, encouragement and direction for *while you are waiting.*

"Get busy living or get busy dying."
—Stephen King

Every heart's desire is in you for a reason and the pursuit of those desires can make life exciting!

Chapter One

While
You Are
Waiting

Discover Who God Is
and What He Does

*"For I know the plans I have for you," declares the Lord,
"plans to prosper you and not to harm you, plans to give
you hope and a future."*

Jeremiah 29:11 NIV

It can be difficult to believe that God has a plan and a purpose for your life if you don't know who God is or who He is to you. As a child in a Christian home, I grew up thinking I knew who God was. I thought: *He's the boss of all bosses, the one who has the final say, the one who watches your every move to determine if you were going to heaven or hell. He was there when things were good but if you did something wrong, He would distance Himself from you, withholding His love or blessings until you were good again.* To me, it was as if your behavior determined His behavior. This is something I used to struggle with, but now realize that my behavior does not make

Him more or less of who He is. **This is NOT who God is and this is NOT what He does.**

Through getting to know Him on my own and seeking to hear His voice before the voice of someone else has brought growth in my faith and my character. I have changed my position and my understanding of who He is because of what His word says. We have to choose to stand strong with the strength of His words. He does not waiver. He is faithful and does not change toward us. **His love is constant.** It does not get stronger or weaker based on our actions. His love remains and is stronger than any force our brains could ever understand.

Who is God and what does He do?

In our culture, we identify who we are by our name and what we do. This is what we should do with God. We should identify Him by His name and by what He does. I believe that we have gotten in the habit of identifying God by what He hasn't done for us. This is not the way it is supposed to be. The world that doesn't know who God truly is needs to know who He is and what His word says about Him. That is our responsibility as Christians. It is my opinion, that we have gotten sidetracked or distracted from boasting on God's goodness. As Christians, we need to come together and start sharing the good news of the Gospel—who God is and what He does.

El Shaddai – Lord God Almighty, the All-Sufficient One

In Genesis, we see Abram and Sarai's relationship become strained because of their desire to have children was so strong and Sarai was unable to have children. Abram asks God for a son and God promises to give them children.

> *When Abram was ninety-nine years old, the Lord appeared to him and said, "I am God Almighty; walk before me faithfully and be blameless. Then I will make my covenant between me and you and will greatly increase your numbers."*
>
> *Abram fell facedown, and God said to him, "As for me, this is my covenant with you: You will be the father of many nations. No longer will you be called Abram; your name will be Abraham, for I have made you a father of many nations. I will make you very fruitful; I will make nations of you, and kings will come from you. I will establish my covenant as an everlasting covenant between me and you and your descendants after you for the generations to come, to be your God and the God of your descendants after you."*
>
> *God also said to Abraham, "As for Sarai your wife, you are no longer to call her Sarai; her name will be Sarah. I will bless her and will surely give you a son by her. I will bless her so that she will be the mother of nations; kings of peoples will come from her."*
>
> Genesis 17:1-7, 15 NIV

Through these scriptures, God reveals His character. He shows His love and compassion for Abram. By changing his name from Abram to Abraham and Sarai to Sarah, He changed their identity. Everything that they had known before was the past and needed to be left behind. By establishing a new name for them, He was fulfilling His plan for their lives. Abraham and Sarah were asking

God for one son, for one child, an heir to carry on their family name. God heard their prayers and saw their hearts' desire and He gave them so much more than what they were asking for.

> *Abraham fell facedown; he laughed and said to himself, "Will a son be born to a man a hundred years old? Will Sarah bear a child at the age of ninety?" And Abraham said to God, "If only Ishmael might live under your blessing!" Then God said, "Yes, but your wife Sarah will bear you a son, and you will call him Isaac. I will establish my covenant with him as an everlasting covenant for his descendants after him. And as for Ishmael, I have heard you: I will surely bless him; I will make him fruitful and will greatly increase his numbers. He will be the father of twelve rulers, and I will make him into a great nation. But my covenant I will establish with Isaac, whom Sarah will bear to you by this time next year." When he had finished speaking with Abraham, God went up from him.*

> Genesis 17:16-22 NIV

Sarah was tired of waiting for God to fulfill His promise and she took matters into her own hands. She convinced Abraham to have children with Hagar. Hagar, who was a slave in their household, had a son with Abraham and named him Ishmael. **Consequences that come from an inability to wait well are often costlier and more damaging than we think.** Abraham and Sarah discovered how complicated it can get and had to learn to wait while they believed for a son. They proved that rushing the waiting process can be a bigger nightmare than an undeveloped dream.

Hagar belittled Sarah for her inability to have children. Ishmael was not the only complication, now Sarah had to deal with Hagar's attitude. Even after they tried to make it happen on their own, Sarah and Abraham had to work through the frustrations that their choices brought into their lives. In the midst of arguments and trying to fix their own mistakes, they were reminded to hold onto the promises of God. They learned and had to believe that what God said would happen.

Jehovah Jireh—The Lord Will Provide

I am thankful to be able to look at my life and bear witness to the goodness of God in every area. I have seen His faithful hand provide when the situation looked bleak or impossible. I am thankful that I can trust God to provide regardless of the situation, He has proven to be faithful over and over again.

As a teenager, I had the opportunity to go to Russia on a several mission trips. Our team was working with orphaned children and created a curriculum like vacation Bible school, with sports, drama and crafts. Through drama and crafts we shared about Jesus and what He had done for all of us. We shared that through our relationship with God and accepting His love, we were able to share that love with them. It was amazing to see the children gain a better understanding of God and His love for them.

On my third missions' opportunity to Russia, we expanded and hosted the vacation Bible school curriculum in Romania. Staying overseas for an additional two weeks after Russia, would mean that before I could go, I would need to raise twice as much support as I had for previous trips. It was in this opportunity, and believing that I was to help our team in Romania, that my faith and trust in God to supply became very, very real.

Before websites and online giving became an option for supporting missions, people used to write support letters. I did this for all of my mission trips. The letter for my third trip did not generate as much support as what was needed. Initially, about half of what was needed came in. Then the responses to the support letter stopped coming. With only half of the support raised, I felt like my friends and family members gave all they could give and I couldn't ask them to give again. I was doing odd jobs like babysitting and giving a majority of my paychecks to the remaining balance for my trip. With a few weeks left before the deadline, in a desperate attempt for help, I made a phone call and explained my position and the lack of funding for the trip. As the phone call was ending, I was faced with the largest dilemma a young adult could face.

I was given the opportunity to speak with a select group of people and present to them my opportunity to serve on the mission trip to Russia and Romania. At the end of the presentation I could request donations from this group in hopes of coming up with the balance due in three weeks. Most would think that it was public speaking that would give me the dilemma, but that was not the case. I was asked to speak to a group of people with whom I did not fundamentally agree with their position or core values. To speak to them and plead for donations would mean that I would need to compromise on some of my core values. Even now, I can remember the almost panicked feeling I had at the end of the conversation. **How could I accept this opportunity?** *How do I make this decision? How could I believe and live by my core values but then compromise for what might come in from donations at the end of the meeting?*

From this situation, I learned how to ask God for wisdom and then experienced receiving it. All I had to do was ask Him and listen for Him to speak to my heart. I learned to get Godly counsel from those I can trust. It is beneficial to get a second opinion or ask questions on issues with which you are unfamiliar, or are more complex than you are comfortable handling alone.

> *For the Lord gives wisdom, from his mouth come knowledge and understanding. He holds success in store for the upright, he is a shield to those whose walk is blameless, for he guards the course of the just and protects the way of his faithful ones.*
>
> Proverbs 2:6-8 NIV

> *The way of fools seems right to them, but the wise listen to advice.*
>
> Proverbs 12:15 NIV

> *Whoever heeds life-giving correction will be at home among the wise.*
>
> Proverbs 15:31 NIV

> *Better a poor but wise youth than an old but foolish king who no longer knows how to heed a warning.*
>
> Ecclesiastes 4:13 NIV

As soon as the offer for the meeting was made, I felt uncomfortable and nervous. I didn't have to wait for the Holy Spirit to tell me it was not a good idea to consider. I also knew that I needed Godly counsel and how to say no and not damage the relationship. I have to admit I was torn. I knew that this speaking engagement was not the solution but I also did not have a solution that would supply the remaining balance for the trip.

After getting off the phone from this call, I made another phone call. I sought Godly advice, counsel, and wisdom. I explained the speaking engagement and the situation. I explained how I believed it would violate my core values and I received confirmation that my instinct or feelings were correct. The wise counsel I received helped me to trust that God would provide and that God would not ask me to go against what I believed in order to go on the trip. Before the phone call was over, we prayed together and agreed to believe God would make a way where there seemed to be no way.

> God would provide. God would not ask me to go against what I believed to obtain provision.

I was three weeks from the deadline and not any closer to coming up with $1200. I tried to believe that it was all going to work out but with each and every passing day, the strength to wait well got weaker and weaker. Time flew quickly and I had one week until the final deadline. I was sitting in a team meeting when my phone rang. I excused myself from the meeting and answered the call. It was a donor, letting me know that they would sponsor my trip. They were sending a check for $1000! I nearly screamed and then started to cry. They were a huge help and encouraged me to believe God for the last little bit. I knew in that moment my trip was going to be completely paid for just in time. I knew because my last paycheck would be enough to cover the remaining balance.

The entire trip was funded! Not only that, but just before leaving, people gave me money so that while I was on the trip I could pick up souvenirs and bring gifts home. I was overwhelmed through this experience. God honored my faithfulness to His calling, made a way where there seemed to be no way, and then went above and beyond.

For this reason, I kneel before the Father, from whom every family in heaven and on earth derives its name. I pray that out of his glorious riches he may strengthen you with power through his Spirit in your inner being, so that Christ may dwell in your hearts through faith. And I pray that you, being rooted and established in love, may have power, together with all the Lord's holy people, to grasp how wide and long and high and deep is the love of Christ, and to know this love that surpasses knowledge—that you may be filled to the measure of all the fullness of God. Now to him who is able to do immeasurably more than all we ask or imagine, according to his power that is at work within us, to him be glory in the church and in Christ Jesus throughout all generations, for ever and ever! Amen.

Ephesians 3:14-21 NIV

God's faithfulness is always on display. In every aspect of life, you can see His hand moving. This can sound challenging, but looking for where and how He is moving is a great way to get our focus off our own circumstances and look for the display of His mighty hands.

Abraham and Sarah tried for years to conceive, and they were unsuccessful. Finally, after all of their unsuccessful years of trying to have a baby on their own, God promised they would have a son within one year (Genesis 17:21 NIV). God honored His word and they had a son. In Genesis 22, God asked Abraham to take his son Isaac and sacrifice him. In obedience, Abraham and Isaac got the wood and the fire ready for the sacrifice. Isaac even asked his father where the lamb for the sacrifice was and Abraham boldly responded in verse eight, *"God himself will provide the lamb for the burnt offering, my son."*

Just as Abraham knew that God would provide, we need to know and believe that God will provide. Abraham drew his knife and raised it over his only son and just as he did that an angel of the Lord appeared.

> *"Do not lay a hand on the boy," he said. "Do not do anything to him. Now I know that you fear God, because you have not withheld from me your son, your only son."*
>
> *Abraham looked up and there in a thicket he saw a ram caught by its horns. He went over and took the ram and sacrificed it as a burnt offering instead of his son. So Abraham called that place The Lord Will Provide. And to this day it is said, "On the mountain of the Lord it will be provided."*
>
> Genesis 22:12-14 NIV

Thankfully, it was Abraham's willingness to obey more than the act of obedience that God was looking for that day. This is a great example of God's character and nature. Abraham and Sarah wanted a son more than anything. They had already acquired wealth and status, but a son was their hearts' desire. As God honors His word and fulfills our heart's desire, it is important to keep the gift in perspective. God is the giver and the provider, and we should never love or covet the gift more than the giver.

Jehovah Rapha—The Lord Who Heals

Growing up, I attended "Healing Crusades" that my grandparents led with a staff and a large team of volunteers. They filled arenas, football fields, stadiums and convention centers around the world. Sick people, caregivers and people who wanted to see God move through signs and wonders attended every service they hosted. I grew up believing God can heal people as we pray in Jesus' name. I not only believed it, I got to witness it too. I believe without a doubt that God can heal the sick.

> He said, "If you listen carefully to the Lord your God and do what is right in his eyes, if you pay attention to his commands and keep all his decrees, I will not bring on you any of the diseases I brought on the Egyptians, for I am the Lord, who heals you."
>
> Exodus 15:26 NIV

Moses had led the Israelites out of Egypt after the plagues God had released on the Egyptians. The plagues brought in sickness, infestations and death. The Israelites witnessed God's protection over them. Every plague that came affected the Egyptians but it did not touch the Israelites. The Israelites saw God's power and might and understood what the Egyptians had gone through. They could see God as their deliverer and healer. He is not a God who gives sickness, disease or harsh circumstances to those who love Him and serve Him.

"But I will restore you to health and heal your wounds," *declares the Lord.*

Jeremiah 30:17 NIV

I have personally experienced being healed. I have seen hundreds if not more, be healed in Jesus' name. It is not something that I can perform or force to happen. I believe by faith, when we pray in the name of Jesus, people are healed.

I am a fourth generation Christian and third generation in ministry. My grandparents, Charles and Frances Hunter, changed everything they did in order to start telling the world about God and the love of Jesus. I have spent a good portion of time referencing who God is with scriptures and examples. He is the same in the past, present and the future. He remains faithful and His character is unchanging. I want you to know who God has been throughout so many generations. I want you to see that He is who He says He is. He is the Great I AM, the all sufficient one, the shepherd who gently guides us, our provider, our healer, the name above all names and the King above all kings.

> Pursue all that He has in store for you and wait well while it all comes together.

God has an amazing plan and purpose for your life. I want to encourage you to pursue all that He has in store for you—wait well while it all comes together. It is important to remember that we are working with God in the plans and purpose He has for our lives. It is not that we leave it all up to Him, like some leave it all to chance. Just as God is intentional with His plan and purpose for our lives, we need to be intentional with our actions and growth in His plan.

My Prayer For You

This is my prayer for you as you discover who God is to you:

Heavenly Father,

I ask that you make yourself known in the lives of my friends. I pray that as they start to trust you that you will reveal yourself in a greater way. I ask that you make yourself known in their lives, their family, their relationships, where they work and where they live. I pray and agree with them that you will show them your plans and purpose for their lives. I pray that you make them strong when they feel weak, make them feel loved when they feel unloved, and help them see the purpose that you have placed inside of them. I pray that they will have a new passion for getting to know you and if they do not already know you, that they would start a relationship with you today. In Jesus' name, amen.

If you would like to start a relationship with God today, it is as easy as asking Jesus into your heart. You can say this: "Jesus, I have sinned. I am sorry for the things that I have done wrong and done against you. Take my sins from me and put them on the cross. Jesus, I need you to come into my life, to lead me and guide me, and show me the plan you have for me. I confess with my mouth and believe in my heart that you are God, in Jesus' name, amen."

It is through Jesus that we can have a relationship with God. Now that you have read this and asked Jesus into your heart, you are a Christian. You will want to know more about God and how to have a relationship with Him. Start by getting a Bible. Take time and look through the different versions to see which one you like and understand the best. Throughout this book I reference the New International Version (NIV) because it is the most commonly used translation and the easiest for me to understand.

Chapter Two

While
You Are
Waiting

Discover The Desires
of Your Heart

May he give you the desire of your heart and make all your plans succeed.

Psalm 20:4 NIV

Take delight in the Lord, and he will give you the desires of your heart.

Psalm 37:4 NIV

I am not sure there is anything more complicated than desires of the heart. They can change, be inconsistent, cause misery or happiness, fulfillment or torture. Often they are well protected— not shared beyond a close friend or spouse. Sometimes we are bold and shere them beyond just the few we trust. At a young age, a heart's desire can be dramatic and impulsive. Later, you realize it is really just a short-term crush, not a crucial heart's desire. A childish heart's desire could also be a craving to become famous, to make it out of a small town, or to drive an extravagant or expensive car. As we grow up, our heart's desire longs for something greater or for more significance.

I grew up in Dallas, Texas. I lived in a nice neighborhood and went to a private school from elementary through high school graduation. It was a posh bubble of brand names and new cars. There was always a feeling of competition in high school for who had the nicest car, the newest car, the most expensive clothing, or the highest priced dress at Prom. **For me, it was a competition that didn't end when I graduated. I continued to strive for attention and lived way beyond what I could afford.**

- ❧ Take a moment and make a list of the things you want to accomplish, create, or attain in your life.

- ❧ Write down the earliest possible memory you have regarding each thing.

- ❧ What circumstances surrounded your decision to want each one of them to be a part of your life?

- ❧ What people, places or things have influenced you to want each of them enough to consider it a "heart's desire"?

- ❧ Are you surprised by the very first thing that came to your mind?

- ❧ What heart's desires came to mind that you are not willing to share with anyone?

- ✍ Would it be wrong for you to have them fulfilled?

- ✍ How do you feel about each heart's desire?

- ✍ Are they worth waiting for?

- ✍ Are they worth waiting well for?

- ✍ Are they worth your time, energy and effort?

- ✍ It their value high enough to spend what is required in order to attain them?

After graduating high school, I went shopping way more than I should. I was always watching for sales at my favorite stores and loved to show up anywhere, even if it was just a church service, in new clothes, with a new purse or jewelry. I liked the attention that I received when people noticed I had something new. This attention created a feeling and this feeling fed my desire to buy more and more things. I bought so many things I could not afford. I created a lifestyle almost impossible to get out of and difficult to maintain. I got into credit card debt and was in over my head. For months and some years, I was only able to pay the minimums. For longer than I would like to admit, I spent available credit, not available cash.

I discovered this was an unhealthy heart's desire and a debt load that I could no longer carry; I started to shop less and less. I could not stop cold turkey, but I did start to value myself enough to know that it wasn't what I had that made me a great person or a good friend. It was my character, how I lived and loved those around me, that gave me value. I acknowledged the root cause was the desire to fit in. This desire was not part of my life's purpose and I had to get it out of my life before it ruined the life I wanted. I had to lay down the need to be noticed for what I had and walk away from the addiction I had created so many years earlier.

It took me a couple of years to get completely out of debt but it was well worth it. Placing a higher value on myself than what labels I was wearing allowed me to grow out of this selfish heart's desire.

What is your heart's desire?

Examine where you are right now. **Do you have a long lasting heart's desire that isn't essential to enjoying your life?** As an adult, I have tried to make better financial choices. I have not always been perfect and I will be the first to admit I have gotten out of debt several times. I have several goals to help me financially. One of which is for my car. I will drive my current car until it has 300,000 miles on it or until I have enough cash to purchase my next car without car payments.

You can create goals that are connected to your heart's desires. A healthy heart's desire that I have is to be a faithful steward with my finances. I believe that as I honor God first with my finances that God will honor my stewardship. Another healthy heart's desire I have is closely connected to giving. Both of these heart's desires line up with who I am and they help me make decisions.

This is where it gets tricky: *What makes you want what you want?* I really like the Cadillac Escalade. I have liked (almost loved) them for longer than I can remember. There is something so special to me about them and I can tell you, I haven't known what it was until recently. I discovered through prayer and analyzing myself the significance of owning an Escalade and what that would mean to me. It would mean that I would have reached an economic status and reached a high enough level of success to afford this car.

For me, getting this car would be a trophy on wheels. I recognize that this heart's desire is rooted in comparison and selfishness. I acknowledged the true root cause of this desire and repented. This wasn't good for me or for my future. I do not want selfishness or comparison in my heart or attached to what my heart desires. After repenting, I have placed this in the category of "nice, but not a heart's desire." I still may drive an Escalade one day—but if I do it will be for the right reason.

Do you have a heart's desire that isn't good for you or for your future?

At the age of thirteen, I was excited to have my first babysitting job. It wasn't too much for me because the parents wanted me to stay inside with their three month old while they did yard work outside. This was the first time I pictured having a family of my own and it made me look forward to the future.

I believe that getting married and having babies is part of God's plan for my life. I have known since a really young age that this is what I wanted. It is my heart's desire and it has stayed more consistent than any other desire, goal or prayer for my life. As I have gotten older, this heart's desire has not changed like other desires have. I know that this is a healthy heart's desire and I remind myself that it is worth the wait. The desire is part of who I am and I am not willing to walk away from it. I have learned and will continue to learn to wait well.

I firmly believe Jeremiah 29:11, that God has a plan and a purpose for my life. I believe that God has a plan and a purpose for every life, whether it is acknowledged or not. It wasn't until a couple of years ago, that my best friend made the comment, "Everyone quotes Jeremiah 29:11, but they stop reading before they read the conditions of finding out the plan and the purpose."

I was guilty of that. I only considered the plan and the purpose, and I did not continue reading to find out the conditions of learning the plan.

> *"For I know the plans I have for you," declares the Lord, "plans to prosper you and not to harm you, plans to give you hope and a future. Then you will call on me and come and pray to me, and I will listen to you. You will seek me and find me when you seek me with all your heart."*
>
> Jeremiah 29:11-13 NIV

In the context of the plan and purpose, we need to seek God to reveal Himself to us. We need to pursue Him more than we seek after the desires of our heart. When we know God, read His word and pursue Him, then the clarity and direction of His plans become evident in our lives.

What does "calling on Him" look like? Calling on God means to talk or pray to Him like you would talk to a friend. You take time to explain the way you feel or what you think and then ask Him to show you what to do next.

When I read the Bible, I can see how God moves and I can hear His heart for my life. When I feel lost or like I don't know what to do, I turn to the Bible. It says in Psalm 119 that His word is a lamp for our feet and a light for our path. Even though the Bible was written a long time ago, it continues to reveal wisdom and insight for how we should live.

My Part, God's Part

In identifying my heart's desires, I have been able to let go of desires that did not pertain to the plan or purpose God has for my life. Through identifying which desires I should hold onto, I have had to create a process that I call "My Part, God's Part".

"My Part" is doing the things that need to be done by the work of my hands, that do not require God's supernatural power to make happen. For example, a desire of my heart is to help people create a structure and processes for their own ministries or companies so that they do not experience harsh learning curves from failures that were avoidable. In order to fulfill this desire, I needed to organize the materials, write the curriculum and then reach the people that need this information the most.

None of these elements require a supernatural act of God in order to make them happen. That does not mean that I keep God out of it. It means that the responsibility of the seminar and creating the curriculum is up to me. The part that is God's part in this example is for Him to move on the hearts and minds of those who hear about this seminar, that they will recognize that this is a great resource for them and the purpose is clear enough to cause them to respond by registering.

Another example for "My Part" and "God's Part" would be this book. It is my heart's desire to encourage people to wait well and believe again. Writing the words, getting editing, proofing, and publishing are all in "My Part." This book showing you how to wait well and believe again is "God's Part." He is with you as you are reading the pages. He is with you when you feel completely alone. He is still with you even when you feel like He has moved on without you. He is with you and the plans and purpose He has for your life will not change but they will always require you to do your part.

Several years ago, a former friend, believed God to be in fulltime ministry. They believed that they needed to be ready and waiting for God to do something. Full time ministry was their heart's desire. They wanted to do what God wanted them to do, but they never got up and out of their house to make anything happen. They chose to stay home and wait on God. They completely believed that God was going to make it happen in spite of them or their circumstances. As each day passed, more and more bills pilled up on the table. Eventually, the threat of water and lights being turned off became a reality. Then the reality of losing their place to live and moving in with family became an example of God not following through and giving them their heart's desire. They understood the "waiting" but they lacked the initiative to work with God to create and maintain the ministry their hearts desired. They opted to only wait for God to do His part and ignored the reality of what was required on their part. God does not work like a magic genie who grants requests and wishes at our command. Accomplishment and fulfillment come from the active partnership between God and us.

Let me make this part clear, God knows the desires of our hearts. He knows what we want, what we need, when we need it and how it is going to happen before we are even aware of the need. In every provision, every dream come true and every accomplishment, something is required of us. Action is required on our part. For a farmer to harvest crops, he must first plant seeds. To gain an income, an employee must do the work. To graduate from school, a student needs to earn passing grades. Examine where you are and what you are doing. **Do you have an active roll in seeing your heart's desire become a reality?**

Detours and Delays

Nothing is worse than running late, then to be in your car and for no reason, traffic is trending like it's 5 pm in Manhattan or Los Angeles. Apply this analogy to your heart's desire and soon frustration, irritation, disappointment and despair can set in. It does not matter how fast or slow time is going, if what you want is not getting any closer to you, emotions will get in the way of waiting well.

No matter how fast or slow time is going, if what you want is not getting any closer to you, emotions will get in the way of waiting well.

Waiting. As soon as it starts to happen, the timer gets set for how long it can last with a good attitude. Have you ever been to dinner with a group of people? Maybe you've just gotten out of church on a Sunday afternoon and your party-of-eight decides to go to lunch together. Welcome to one of my least favorite situations. It never fails, after church on Sunday is one of the worst times to go out to eat. It's like going to the grocery store at 5:30 pm and being shocked that everyone else has decided to go to the store too.

Back to the restaurant, after 45 minutes, your group finally gets a table. Then you're there for a few minutes (it feels like fifteen) before your server comes to the table. The group orders their drinks and the server offers appetizers, you politely decline and say you'll be ready to order when they get back with the drinks. Now more waiting is required. You've only ordered your drinks but what seems like forever has to come and go before they come back with them. Now the drinks are to the table, but the server has left before getting your lunch order. More time passes, and the server finally returns to your table to get the orders. The group is now even hungrier, more frustrated, and slightly crazy, waiting to give their food order.

The order is turned into the kitchen and now more time has passed. The group that started out praising God at church has now reached what is called "hangry." Hangry is the combination of the words hungry and angry. Food comes to the table with the help of two servers. Then with a cranky "finally" voiced from the group, the group prays and begins to eat.

I avoid this situation at all costs. I make it a point to avoid going to dinner in large groups. I have seen this scenario play out several times and I do not want to be a part of it. When I do go, I keep in mind how many other tables our server may have and suggest places that you can pick up your food from the counter.

You may be thinking; what does going to dinner have to do with my heart's desire? For me, it is a simple analogy. How is your attitude different when you ask for something (whether from God or someone around you) and you get it quickly versus when what you ask for takes a while or even years to receive it?

Detours and delays that cause a reroute to our lives are never enjoyable. There can be even more frustrating situations like striving to get out of debt, but then getting laid off. It can be paying your car off then needing a new engine. It can be the counseling that was made available after too much abuse. There are endless possibilities and variables that can affect the journey of our lives. It is important that in every situation that we remind ourselves to look for the good and to ask God to show us the plan and purpose even in the midst of adversity.

This is how I define waiting well.

> ## WAITING WELL:
> **Maintaining a positive attitude and outlook for the duration of time spent while a favorable outcome, answered prayer, or heart's desire has yet to be attained or delivered.**

Waiting well does not mean reverse psychology or playing mind games. It is not a "pretend I don't want it then I'll get it" mindset. It is to believe God at His word, that He wants our hearts' desires to be fulfilled. Believe God for His plans to become your plans. Believe God for His purpose to become your purpose. Believe and live in faith with action according to what you know is your heart's desire, passion and purpose.

Consider Solomon. He could have asked God for anything and what he asked for was the wisdom needed to lead his people.

> *Give me wisdom and knowledge, that I may lead this people, for who is able to govern this great people of yours?" God said to Solomon, "Since this is your heart's desire and you have not asked for wealth, possessions or honor, nor for the death of your enemies, and since you have not asked for a long life but for wisdom and knowledge to govern my people over whom I have made you king, therefore wisdom and knowledge will be given you. And I will also give you wealth, possessions and honor, such as no king who was before you ever had and none after you will have."*
>
> 2 Chronicles 1:10-12 NIV

Consider again, your heart's desires and ask yourself:

- ✂ Am I holding onto unhealthy or foolish desires?

- ✂ Have I called on God, and sought Him for clarity on His plans and purpose of my life? (Jeremiah 29:11-13)

- ✂ Am I waiting well during the detours and delays?

- ✂ How am I waiting well with faith in action?

My Prayer for You

Here is my prayer for you as you ask and discover your part and God's part:

Heavenly Father,

I ask that you help my friends discover all that you have for them. I pray in agreement with them, that they will know the direction you have for their lives. I ask that you reveal and give guidance in the areas of their life that they need to take action and develop. I pray that you give them wisdom and understanding to know what is their part and what is your part. I ask that as they take initiative and start accepting the responsibility for their part, that you would honor and bless their efforts. Thank you for new ideas, creativity, insight, and knowledge for my friends in Jesus' name, amen.

Questions to Consider

- ☞ What are my heart's desires?

- ☞ How long have I had these desires?

- ☞ What do I know I need to do that is my part?

- ☞ What do I need God to do that is His part?

- ☞ In what areas am I waiting well?

- ☞ In what areas do I need to improve or take action in order to wait well?

Waiting well requires
me to believe and live
in faith with action
according to what I know
is my heart's desire,
passion and purpose.

Chapter Three

While You Are Waiting

Grow Where You Are

One of the best things you can do for yourself is acknowledge that you have a lot to offer this world. Without you, there would be lives that would be incomplete, joyless, and suffering from a void they didn't know how to fill. You have gifts inside you that you need to share with the world.

Regardless of what you are waiting for, don't wait to live your life. I often share and speak on enjoying the moment. Life will pass you by and hitting the pause button until you achieve a certain status or accomplishment does not stop time from moving forward. If you hit pause, you will miss out on some of the best moments of your life.

While you are waiting, improve your environment.

Take some time and examine where you are right now. Have you created an environment around you that will allow growth or allow what you are waiting for to arrive?

At this moment, I am writing and sharing my experiences and observations as well as what I have learned—to enjoy my life regardless of the season. I try to take inventory of my life and see where I am investing my time, talent and treasure, to make sure I am doing the best with what I have. I have looked at my life and have seen areas and activities that required too much of my time. There were areas that consumed too much and also several areas of my life that I was ignoring.

It is important to restore balance to your life as a way of inviting enjoyment into your life. If you find that certain aspects of your life are requiring too much of you and the return on your investment is low, consider making arrangements to bring that commitment to an end. If you have found that you love doing one particular thing but do not get to do it often enough, then make arrangements in your schedule and adjust your commitments to do more of what brings you fulfillment. Life has a way of getting out of balance and if we forget to take an inventory of where we are spending our lives, we will look back and face regret of time mismanaged and opportunities lost.

Consider where you are right now. Do you have an environment conducive to allowing what you are waiting for to come into your life? Have you made room for what you are waiting for in your life?

After I asked myself these very same questions, I had to make adjustments and adapt my focus. I lost too much time to things or people I could not change. I lost sleep over relationships that no matter how much I poured into them or lowered my expectations, I was still getting hurt. I found out I could only give so much and could only go on like that for so long.

Realizing the detriment I was becoming to my own happiness, I made changes. I would like to encourage you to do the same. Spend some time evaluating where you are and where you want to be. Are there things in your life that are blocking you from growing or from attaining what you want? Remove familiar comfort zones and improve your environment. You may need to change your physical environment or you may need to change the relationships you allow in your environment.

> Spend some time evaluating where you are and where you want to be.

One of the greatest advantages of moving to a new environment is the ability to start fresh and be who you want to be. You get to start with a clean slate with people around you, a new job, a new community, and new neighbors and so on. For some, the history that they have or the way they have been perceived makes it nearly impossible to let bygones be bygones. I have found that once a person hits the extreme limits of being hurt or being taken advantage of, the only solution becomes starting over in a new place.

Escaping or leaving to avoid resolving the issues is not what I am suggesting or what I am trying to say. What I am saying is, if you have reached the point of no return and no growth, the viable option becomes leaving and starting over.

The down side to starting over is all of the new relationships that will also start from scratch. You'll find a new place to live, work, worship, and shop. Every relationship will start with the basics and require a new time frame of waiting. Waiting to feel like it's home. Waiting to feel the friendships are genuine. Waiting to go from an entry-level job to earning the next promotion.

This is why it is important to take inventory of your life on a regular basis. Inventory will allow you to see what areas need attention. Regular maintenance often makes adjustments smaller and less painful. It will allow you to see and make adjustments before anything gets beyond repair or to an extreme.

Ask yourself this question: *am I tired of being where I am and am I ready to do something different? Will I take the time to inventory my life? When will I make the adjustments needed in order to be more fulfilled in what I do, where I work and where I live?*

While you're waiting, evaluate those around you.

I believe you can tell a lot about a person by the friends they keep and specifically, the ones they keep the closest to them. John C. Maxwell, in the book, *The 21 Irrefutable Laws of Leadership* (Law 11) wrote The Law of the Inner Circle. The subtitle of the chapter is "A Leader's Potential Is Determined by Those Closest to Him."

I have read this book several times and have also listened to the audio book. This is and probably will always be one of my top three favorite laws. The first time I read it I took an immediate look at my inner circle. Who was I allowing to speak directly into my life and were they qualified to hold this position? That can sound really harsh or even hurtful, but it is not meant to be. It is a protective question that will allow you to evaluate those you have kept closest to you.

If your inner circle is not filled with people who can speak the truth to you in love and kindness, look out for your best interest, and help you maintain growth in every area of your life, you need to create an exchange in your inner circle. You need people who believe in you but can also help you know that you are making the best decisions and can help you maintain or even create balance in your life. This select group of people can also tell you "no" to an idea or to a plan you have and you will listen to their discernment. Again, this is a select group of people who are looking out for your best interest, so when they say "no" it is because of love or protection, not jealousy or malice. Understand the complete purpose of the inner circle. I made changes to mine and it has helped me grow as a leader, a speaker, a writer, a friend and even as a Christian.

> He who walks with wise men will be wise, but the companion of fools will suffer harm.
>
> Proverbs 13:20 NIV

> Do not associate with a man given to anger; or go with a hot-tempered man, or you will learn his ways and find a snare for yourself.
>
> Proverbs 22:24-25 NIV

"Do not be deceived: 'Bad company corrupts good morals.'"

1 Corinthians 15:33 NIV

I am thankful I have not had to completely leave friends behind. I did, however, make changes to those I allowed access to my life and my time. I was sick for almost two years and was doing what I could to get better. One of the things that my doctor highly recommended was avoiding unnecessary bad news. I nicknamed them "Bad News Bears."

"Bad News Bears" are people who share or repeat bad news that has nothing to do with you and it is something you cannot do anything about. You are a set of ears that gets forced to listen to information regarding someone else's crisis, drama, disappointment or unfortunate news. You are also not the only person with whom the Bad News Bear is sharing this. You just happen to be in the line up of several people to hear the report shared by the Bear.

Avoiding and addressing the Bad News Bear can be difficult at first but there is hope. Once you have addressed the issue, you won't have to address it very often and your world will become less polluted by the unnecessary bad news toxins. Addressing the Bears will not completely eliminate bad news from your life, but it will greatly reduce the amount of negativity in your growth environment.

Preparing your life to receive what you have been waiting for includes releasing relationships that will keep you stuck where you are.

Preparing your life to receive what you have been waiting for includes releasing relationships that will keep you stuck where you are. Ask yourself:

- ॐ How do the relationships closest to me hurt or help my purpose to be fulfilled?

- ॐ How do these relationships hinder or assist me in preparing my environment to receive?

Hopefully your answers will help you consider making adjustments to your life and their proximity to you.

Just as it is important to remove negative voices from your surroundings, it is equally important to replace those voices with someone or something positive. I am certified as a speaker and coach with The John Maxwell Team. In addition to the training I have received, one of the things I appreciate most about my certification is the group of mentors that are available to me. They are several years ahead of me in speaking, teaching, coaching, and mentoring. They each have their own companies and have developed leaders who add value to their sphere of influence every single day. I want to learn more from them because they have achieved something similar to what I want to achieve. Beyond that, I also have friends who are life coaches, motivational speakers, and experts in their field that I can call and ask questions and gain guidance.

It is important to replace your negative thoughts and messages with positive thoughts and positive messages. Move from "I can't" thoughts and statements into "I will try" and "I will try again." Sometimes we are not able to get to the point of "I did" by ourselves, but the good thing is, we are not meant to do it all by ourselves. We are made to need help and to even need a team.

Life has never been, nor will it be, possible to do alone. This world is filled with gifted and talented people that can help direct you or speak to the purpose in your life. I always recommend that people do research and find people who do what you want to do, work where you want to work, and love how you want to love, and live how you want to live. They have figured out how to do what you want to do and it is okay to get help from them to achieve it. Now, more than ever, life coaching has become popular because people have realized they need help and accountability to attain their heart's desires.

I am convinced that we all need to build the drive or force needed to unlock our potential and go for what we want. You may not feel like you have it in you, but I am certain, you can find someone to help you identify the value that is in you and help you discover how to get it out.

While you are waiting, find forgiveness and restore relationships.

Restoring friendships or relationships can be one of the hardest things a person could choose to go through. It could be the hardest, but it could also be the biggest benefit you could welcome into your life.

My parents divorced when I was a senior in high school. There are a number of contributing factors that led to their divorce. Ultimately, when it was finalized I was devastated and blamed my dad for all of it. Allow me to share this journey with you.

For years, I thought my dad was totally at fault. I couldn't or didn't want to even talk to him because of how hurt I was. I had no compassion for him or his position. He would call or text and I would take my time to get back to him. He made several efforts to stay connected with me and because I was so hurt, I felt like he wasn't being genuine and was putting on a show. As time passed, he slowly stopped calling as often and the texts stopped coming as well. Once he stopped, I reduced any remaining expectations I had of him and almost completely locked him out of my life.

I reduced my relationship with my dad to the text messages sent on his birthday or Christmas. I felt so hurt for so long that I felt that doing this would spare me of future pain from this relationship. I even went as far as asking one of my brothers-in-law to walk me down the aisle when I get married. I had decided that my dad didn't deserve the honor or the privilege of giving me to my future husband. I relinquished all expectations and understood that whatever my dad did to make an effort wouldn't be enough to make everything better.

I reduced my relationship and expectations of my earthly father. In lowering my expectations in the natural, I increased them in the supernatural. I desired and craved a strong and personal relationship with God the Father. The way I looked at God changed and I was able to see Him as my provider, my healer, my comforter, and the One who would make all things come together in my life. In this, I have grown up trusting God to meet every need that I have and have chosen to listen to His voice over my life and no one else's.

Somewhere in the last couple of years I have started to make more of an effort to communicate with my dad. I haven't blown up his phone with text messages or even called him once a month.

When I think about him, I hope that he is doing well and that he is happy and healthy. I randomly text him and he texts or calls me too. I pray for him and most importantly, I have forgiven him for how hurt I felt.

Valentine's weekend February 2015, I was within an hour of Dallas/Ft. Worth where my dad lives. I called him and set up a time to go over to his house. I remember this trip like it was only a week ago. My best friend was with me, and I am so thankful she witnessed this significant conversation between me and my father. The time spent with him brought an immeasurable amount of healing to my heart and to his as well. We spent so much time talking about real issues and through open communication with consideration for what we believe, how we live, and what we do, we were able to find forgiveness for each other and bring restoration to our relationship. Where my heart was hardened, God has softened my heart toward him and I now have a greater ability to love him and show him compassion.

While we were talking, he shared the details of his battles with cancer. In his consultation he told his doctor that the cancer would not keep him from walking all four of his beautiful daughters down the aisle. As he shared this he got teary-eyed and it hit my heart. He said, "And when it's time, I would like to walk you down the aisle if you would let me." And I said through tears and a whisper, "I will let you walk me down the aisle."

> "Jesus said to his disciples: 'Things that cause people to stumble are bound to come, but woe to anyone through whom they come. It would be better for them to be thrown into the sea with a millstone tied around their neck than to

cause one of these little ones to stumble. So watch yourselves. If your brother or sister sins against you, rebuke them; and if they repent, forgive them. Even if they sin against you seven times in a day and seven times come back to you saying 'I repent,' you must forgive them.'"

Luke 17:1-4 NIV

I am sure that just as much as I felt hurt by my dad, he felt hurt by me. In our conversation, we were able to forgive and be forgiven for the hurts we caused each other. I know that forgiveness and restoration to this relationship is one step in the direction of attaining my heart's desires. Our participation was required in order to see God bring healing to the relationship. I also believe that it was a turning point in seeing God cause things to work together for my good (Romans 8:28).

While you are waiting, you might get tired but don't give up.

I know the waiting room is a tough place to be. I was recently speaking at a conference and one of the other speakers shared on her development of patience. She joked that God could give her patience and He could do it quickly. For the next three days, I hit moment after moment of patience practicing opportunities. It's like they didn't end. I was stuck driving behind a slow car. Later I was in line behind someone who had no idea where they were going or what they were doing. Then it seemed as if it became one thing after another. Thinking about it now still makes me shake my head with the disbelief of the patience that I needed to have during that time period.

Then to top it all off, I am writing a book about "waiting well." This is nothing short of or other than character development every single day. Waiting on any level can be difficult, but for me, it seems even harder when I feel like there is no reason to wait. The back up or delay is for no reason and it clearly feels like a waste of time. Be encouraged! You can wait well even in those moments or you can allow yourself to get frustrated and discouraged. Allowing frustration and discouragement to set in can make the waiting room more unbearable. The good news is, **how you wait is entirely up to you.**

> *Many are the afflictions of the righteous, but the LORD delivers him out of them all.*
>
> Psalm 34:19 NIV

> *"Do not fear, for I am with you; Do not anxiously look about you, for I am your God I will strengthen you, surely I will help you, Surely I will uphold you with My righteous right hand."*
>
> Isaiah 41:10 NIV

Being tired or getting tired of waiting happens, but do not give up on what you want because you feel like it has been too long. Everything that you are reading right now is hopefully directing you to wait for what your heart wants. It's a desire that is in you for a purpose. Examining the different areas of your life, evaluating friendships, restoring relationships and forgiving yourself or others, is all part of protecting the purpose inside you while creating the atmosphere to receive that for which you have been hoping, believing and waiting.

> *Therefore, my beloved brethren, be steadfast, immovable, always abounding in the work of the Lord, knowing that your toil is not in vain in the Lord.*

> 1 Corinthians 15:58 NIV

Writing this makes me think of the song by Journey, "Don't Stop Believin'." With everything in me, I believe God does amazing things everyday and most of the time He uses you and me to make them happen. Whatever you are waiting for, you have waited long enough to not give up. Don't stop believing!

While you're waiting, believe everything is possible.

There are several areas of my life that have been in the waiting room for a while. It is probably how I have the idea to wait well. I know that I have struggled with believing God for what His word says, but I have also been overwhelmed with His faithfulness and timely provision in my life. I have struggled with asking for something in prayer while also thinking He may not do it or even worse, that He may not be able to do it.

> *Jesus asked the boy's father, "How long has he been like this?"*

> *"From childhood," he answered. "It has often thrown him into fire or water to kill him. But if you can do anything, take pity on us and help us."*

"If you can'?" said Jesus. "Everything is possible for one who believes."

Immediately the boy's father exclaimed, "I do believe; help me overcome my unbelief!"

When Jesus saw that a crowd was running to the scene, he rebuked the impure spirit. "You deaf and mute spirit," he said, "I command you, come out of him and never enter him again."

Mark 9:21-25 NIV

The boy was healed and the impure spirit never bothered him or entered him again. In the same manner, I have confronted my disbelief head on and want to encourage you to do the same. It is not wrong to have thoughts of disbelief or lack of faith, but to allow them to stay, will corrupt your ability to trust God and wait well for what you believe to receive.

While you're waiting, do not worry.

I tell you the truth, I have not always been so confident while I'm waiting. I have worried about waiting. I have worried that I will wait so long for things my heart desires, that what I want will happen after it's too late. "Too late" is like listening to Alanis Morrissette sing "Ironic."

An old man turned ninety-eight
He won the lottery and died the next day
It's a black fly in your Chardonnay
It's a death row pardon two minutes too late

Isn't it ironic, don't you think
It's like rain on your wedding day
It's a free ride when you've already paid
It's the good advice that you just didn't take
Who would've thought, it figures

Too late is like:

- trying to pay off debt after the car has been repossessed,

- sunscreen applied after the skin is burned,

- checking the oil after the engine is fried.

To each of these scenarios, the time period before the final straw is drawn is a certain amount of time. **The time frame is different for everyone but more good would be done in preventative care than in worrying about how much time you have until it is too late.**

Worry robs us of our joy today and ruins the anticipation for tomorrow. Instead of replaying this hit song, look at the other options and do what is best for you. Consider the choices that will make your life better and more fulfilling. I remind myself to trust God and I would like to do the same for you. When worrying is taking up your time, there are three options that come to mind:

1. Stop waiting and give up on what you want.

2. Worry about the time spent waiting
   and lose joy of everyday life.

3.   Wait well and trust God's faithfulness
     with the desires of you heart.

What will you choose?

"Therefore I tell you, do not worry about your life, what you will eat or drink; or about your body, what you will wear. Is not life more than food, and the body more than clothes? Look at the birds of the air; they do not sow or reap or store away in barns, and yet your heavenly Father feeds them. Are you not much more valuable than they? Can any one of you by worrying add a single hour to your life?

"And why do you worry about clothes? See how the flowers of the field grow. They do not labor or spin. Yet I tell you that not even Solomon in all his splendor was dressed like one of these. If that is how God clothes the grass of the field, which is here today and tomorrow is thrown into the fire, will he not much more clothe you—you of little faith?

"So do not worry, saying, 'What shall we eat?' or 'What shall we drink?' or 'What shall we wear?' For the pagans run after all these things, and your heavenly Father knows that you need them.

"But seek first his kingdom and his righteousness, and all these things will be given to you as well. Therefore do not worry about tomorrow, for tomorrow will worry about itself. Each day has enough trouble of its own."

Matthew 6:25-34 NIV

So I return to the thought and the belief that everything is possible. I choose to believe God's word over my life and I hope that you will too. I hope that you find this thought to be contagious and that you write it on your wall to remind yourself every single day: **EVERYTHING IS POSSIBLE!**

> *"For I am confident of this very thing, that He who began a good work in you will perfect it until the day of Christ Jesus."*
>
> Philippians 1:6 NIV

> *"I can do all things through Him who strengthens me."*
>
> Philippians 4:13 NIV

> *"And we know that God causes all things to work together for good to those who love God, to those who are called according to His purpose."*
>
> Romans 8:28 NIV

> *"'Do not fear, for I am with you; Do not anxiously look about you, for I am your God I will strengthen you, surely I will help you, Surely I will uphold you with My righteous right hand.'"*
>
> Isaiah 41:10 NIV

My Prayer for You

This is my prayer for you while you grow where you are:

Heavenly Father,

I come before you today to ask that you encourage my friends while they grow where they are. Help them see the friendships that need evaluation, their attitudes that could use adjusting and overall, help them stand firm and trust you for their heart's desire. Father, I ask that you would speak life to their dreams, give courage and bravery to pursue their heart's desire but also give them ability to wait well where the right time has not yet come. In Jesus' name, I ask that any doubt or worry would go from their heart and mind. I thank you for giving them peace as they wait on your hand to move and guide them. In Jesus' name, amen.

Questions To Consider

- ✍ Are you tired of being where you are and ready to do something different?

- ✍ What changes need to be made to your existing inner circle?

- ✍ Do you need to create your inner circle?

- ✍ What relationships need restoration or forgiveness?

- ✍ What will you do to cause restoration or forgiveness to take place?

ॐ   Do you find yourself worrying throughout the day?

ॐ   What causes you to worry?

ॐ   What can you do to resolve the issues
     that cause you to worry?

Protect the purpose
inside you while you
create the atmosphere to
receive that which you
have been waiting for.

Chapter Four

While
You Are
Waiting

... to Get Married

I want to warn you; I have brave faith. I believe God for His best and for every day to be awesome. I often tell people that I wake up with a fresh cup of optimism and faith. No matter what happened yesterday, today is a new day and it is up to me to make the best of it.

With that said, I can tell you that with my fresh and overflowing cup of optimism, I expect the best and believe EVERYTHING IS POSSIBLE. I hope you find this more contagious than annoying. I believe God can do all things and I expect for Him to show off in a big way for those whom He loves and who love Him. I also know that I need to show up in my own life and not avoid the future.

Over the past several years, I have become a bit of a planner. I like to know the details and plan my day. Usually, I plan the next three days to a week ahead. Some occasions or events make me plan months in advance. Either way, I like to know what is going on and details are becoming more and more important to me.

When I lived in Dallas and decided to move to Nashville, my sister Charity shared with me some great advice. She encouraged me to start planning the move and to get out of debt before I moved. She explained that I would have the greatest advantage in the fresh start if I moved debt free. The plan and move took two years to accomplish. In the end, I moved with only a school loan debt. I paid off my credit cards, gas card, store cards and my car! It was a huge relief to move and be able to create a fresh start. Nothing was really bad where I was, but it was the feeling of something more and something bigger that was drawing me to Nashville.

Outside of the advantage of a fresh start was the ability to grow as an individual, as a business owner, and start a new circle of friends without the baggage of history that some relationships had. One reason I was happy to move was to choose my new friends wisely. I could see some relationships were not encouraging to my faith or what I was believing God for in my life. I was around a lot of couples who were not happily married. I had taken inventory and the relationships that were closest to me were ones that did not help me maintain hope or expectation for my life. I watched marriages crumble and I was aware that this was not a good environment for me. I witnessed that one spouse was controlling, another was unfaithful, some worked too much, others had spending habits that were breaking up their family. It was too toxic for me to live in and be able to believe that great marriages were possible.

I moved with anticipation and knew that I was going to meet the man of my heart's desire once I moved. Within a few months, I found an amazing church, made new friends, started branching out with my business. Everything was going well. I was hitting goals, growing my clientele, and having fun with my family. The only goal that I wasn't able to achieve was the change in my relationship status. I was years beyond the timeline I created for my life but I knew that what I want was worth the wait. I believe that any amount of time spent waiting is on purpose, for a purpose and will be a good investment for my future.

While you are waiting to get married, keep your faith in action alive.

One day I got an email with a concert notification. One of my favorite bands was playing and the concert was six months away. I knew that I needed to get two tickets for this concert because I would want my boyfriend to have a ticket too. The only problem was I didn't have a boyfriend at that time and I had not met anyone who could be a potential boyfriend. You may think buying two tickets is quite silly, childish or even a waste of money. I can agree with you. I hope you also see that purchasing two tickets was more than just that, it was my faith in action.

> *"What good is it, my brothers and sisters, if someone claims to have faith but has no deeds? Can such faith save them? Suppose a brother or a sister is without clothes and daily food. If one of you says to them, 'Go in peace; keep warm and well fed,' but does nothing about their physical needs, what good is it? In the same way, faith by itself, if it is not*

accompanied by action, is dead. But someone will say, 'You have faith; I have deeds.'

"Show me your faith without deeds, and I will show you my faith by my deeds. You believe that there is one God. Good! Even the demons believe that—and shudder. You foolish person, do you want evidence that faith without deeds is useless?

"Was not our father Abraham considered righteous for what he did when he offered his son Isaac on the altar? You see that his faith and his actions were working together, and his faith was made complete by what he did.

"And the scripture was fulfilled that says, 'Abraham believed God, and it was credited to him as righteousness,' and he was called God's friend. You see that a person is considered righteous by what they do and not by faith alone.

"In the same way, was not even Rahab the prostitute considered righteous for what she did when she gave lodging to the spies and sent them off in a different direction?

"As the body without the spirit is dead, so faith without deeds is dead."

James 2:14-26

The concert came and went and to be fully honest, as I love to be, I went to the concert with my sister. I can laugh about it now but I can also be proud of myself for making room for what I believed God for in my life.

While you are waiting to get married, honor yourself.

One night I raced down a freeway in Dallas. My three sisters were all in different cars and had gotten ahead of me while we drove. I sped up trying to catch up to them when all of a sudden a police car was behind me with their lights on. I pulled over and the officer asked me to get out of the car and sit down at a park bench. He instructed me to color in a coloring book. I argued back saying, "This is a waste of time and I am just trying to catch up to my sisters." The officer responded with directions for coloring the pages and said once the pages were completed I was free to go. I took a fistful of colors and scribbled all across the pages. Long, fast strokes, I completely ignored the lines on the page and colored from corner to corner. I colored as quickly as I could so that I could get in the car and go.

Now to be honest, this incident was a dream, but it is a dream that has stuck with me for several years. I believe that God can speak through dreams. Through them, He can give wisdom, direction, and discernment. God can even restore hope and joy through dreams.

In this dream, I believe that God was telling me that I was trying to go faster than what was good for me, that I didn't need to compete or race to catch up to my sisters. My sisters were going at the right pace for their lives. I needed to stop comparing my life to theirs, where I was and where they were. I also believe that there were elements of my life that I was trying to get through too quickly and that paying attention to details would be more beneficial than skipping them all together.

I am one of four girls. All of my sisters are married and have children. At the time of this dream my younger sister, Abigail, had not yet had her son, but she was already married and I was comparing my life to hers. Comparison is a dangerous trap; anyone can fall into it. It's important that once you fall into it that you quickly get out of it. I had to decide to honor myself and live my own life.

Comparison is a dangerous trap.

To honor myself meant to appreciate the qualities that make me who I am. This became possible when I decided to stop comparing my life to those around me. After all, if I believe that God has a plan and a purpose for my life and that He has that for everyone, I must also believe that our plans are not all identical but as unique as we are.

While you are waiting to get married, respect yourself and your sexuality.

It doesn't take a rocket scientist to realize that the day and age in which we are living does not honor or encourage the notion of waiting until marriage to have sex. Our culture does not even encourage people to wait until a second date. The idea of waiting to have sex or anything else has been considered conventional or sheltered. In our modern society, waiting—much less waiting well—is not the way to think or live.

When I was twenty years old I worked in a day care. I was right in the middle of everyone else I worked with, a few were younger and a few were older. At one point, all of the ladies were standing in the hallway and the sex topic came up. Granted, some of the ladies in the conversation were married with children but the rest of the group was either single or in a dating relationship.

One of the girls looked at me and asked if I was sleeping with my boyfriend. I was slow to answer the question, more because I was caught off guard by it. Then I answered, "No, I am not." Her jaw nearly hit the floor and she quickly responded with, "Wait! How old are you?" I told her my age and she said, "I can't believe you're still a virgin ... that's impressive. I wish I would have waited a little longer, but now, there's no point."

This story is such a simple example of what a few years can do. The lady I worked with was three years younger than me. From one age group to the next generation, we are losing a sense of morals and self-respect. The concept of waiting until marriage has become so devalued that fewer and fewer teenagers or young adults find out about waiting until after they have had sex. Instead of it being an honorable decision at a young age, it becomes the result of STDs or too many failed relationships. My heart breaks when I hear reports of sexual acts happening on school buses among middle school and sometimes younger classes. Where are the parents and leaders and why are we not approaching this issue from a stronger and more vocal position?

Recently, I was asked this by a friend; he said, "Would you ever make a huge purchase without doing some research?" I said, "No." Quickly he followed it with "There you go." I came back even quicker and said, "That doesn't mean to have sex before you get married. You're not making a purchase, like buying a car or an appliance." He started laughing and said, "Well, you should know what you're getting into."

My heart sank. This comparison is a common thought process towards sex. Sex is such a small percentage of what the relationship is based on, it should not be part of the qualifying information. Relationships have issues that are more important than sexual compatibility.

Honesty, integrity, communication, spending habits, work ethics, and dependability are topics that should be approached before deciding to have sex with someone you're interested in. Sex, in consideration of how long one session could possibly last, will still be shorter than the conversation needed to figure out what to have for dinner when nothing sounds good. This may be a slight exaggeration, but I am hoping you see the small point I am trying to make. If you are not yet married, I hope you will think a little longer and consider your health, your body and your heart before you climb into bed with someone who may not consider your best interest before their own.

If you haven't started waiting, right now is a good time to start.

It's a given that most parents find it uncomfortable to talk to their children about sex. I haven't had to explain this yet, so I can only imagine from minor questions I have had to answer. Children get curious and their parents should be the first place they look to in order to gain knowledge about their own body.

I remember being in fifth grade and the girls in my grade watched a video at school that explained reproduction, but mostly how the female body worked. Don't get me wrong the video was a helpful resource that was simple to understand and extremely awkward to watch. I remember thinking to myself, *why didn't my mom tell me this stuff?* Later that day, I asked her if she knew about the video and why didn't she tell me we would be watching a video or learning this in school. She explained that she signed a release form and thought it would make it easier to understand how my body was made to work.

It made sense, but I can honestly tell you, I do not remember who explained intercourse to me or who would have taught me to wait until I got married. I know at some point my parents told me it was better to wait until I got married and there had been some reoccurring mentions of it when I was a young teenager, but after that, it wasn't something that I would keep at the forefront of my mind or keep strong in my heart. When I was sixteen, I remember teachers talking about the shame a girl would experience if she got pregnant outside of marriage. They warned us about public shame and harsh judgment instead of understanding the importance of waiting and the sacredness of marriage.

Wherever you are right now, you can start waiting for love that says, "I do and I will, forever." I have friends who chose not to wait to be intimate with each other. She had been raised to wait until marriage, but between her and her boyfriend, they decided they would rather not wait to have sex. They wanted to be with each other regardless of whether or not they would choose to get married. They lived together for a couple of years, then got engaged and then got married. Oddly enough, they chose to not have sex for several weeks before they got married. According to them, they did this so they could make their wedding night special.

I think this is a great way to prepare for the uniqueness of the wedding night, but I also want to encourage you to honor your potential marriage by waiting from the beginning. By doing this, you respect yourself and choose to give them all of your heart, mind and body, on the agreement that they will give you all of those things in return. Marriage is supposed to be a lifetime commitment and waiting for the right person is worth it.

Committing to spend the rest of your lives together is a huge promise to keep. It will require a lifetime of making that same choice everyday. In my opinion, the most beautiful part of waiting to have sex until you get married is the short list of previous partners that you will have to share with your spouse. It is a beautiful gift and you are special enough to save it and give it to the one who deserves to hold your heart in their hand forever.

While you're waiting to get married, live the life you want.

In my early twenties I would often say, "I can't wait to get married because then I can ..." do something that I can't do by myself. I would mostly refer to traveling, because to me, it's more fun to go somewhere with someone then going alone. I said this in front of one of my sisters and she replied, "Don't wait to travel until you get married. Chances are once you are married you won't be able to travel." I heard her say this and instead of arguing I decided I wouldn't wait to do what I wanted to do until I had my husband to go with me.

Traveling is a small example. There are so many options of things to do, places to see, countries to visit, concerts to attend, movies to watch and on and on. I decided years ago that I would not pause my life until I got married. If you pause your life over any circumstances or relationship status, you will find that when you're ready to un-pause it, you have lost both time and opportunities. **Opportunities can sometimes make their way back to you; time never will.** Once time is spent or lost, it's gone. I decided to use my time to live the life I wanted and to make the most of the best opportunities that come my way.

"May you live all the days of your life."
—Jonathan Swift

I remember seeing a movie preview for a movie being released in theaters. I was so excited to see it. When the movie opened, I couldn't find anyone to go with me. One random day, in the middle of the afternoon, I chose to go to the movie theatre by myself. This was one of the toughest and most humbling moments I have ever experienced but it was a moment that strengthened my character. I wasn't going to let the idea of doing it by myself prevent me from doing what I wanted to do.

Thankfully, this isn't something that I have had to do very often, but once I did it, I found out it wasn't as difficult as I thought it would be. Don't miss your opportunity to enjoy your life because of your relationship status. One of the best benefits of enjoying life as a single person is doing something the way you hoped, dreamed or imagined. You do not have to make arrangements around someone else's schedule. Enjoy the moments. Life is too short to wait for someone else in order to live your life. Do what you can to live life to the fullest. Celebrate life with friends and family. Don't look back and wish you had done something different. You have today; do all you can with it.

While you're waiting to get married, get ready.

I have personal philosophy to live by: set yourself up for the best future possible, take care of today, and enjoy tomorrow. This may sound like a fortune cookie or an optimistic frame of mind, but it's one of the best things you can do for yourself. Keep this in mind as you move into the next part of this chapter.

Set yourself up for the best future possible.

There are several issues that are closely related to divorce. The best thing to do is reduce your ability to bring one (or more) of these issues into your marriage. Right now it could be just you that you have to take care of, but imagine you were also responsible for your spouse or even your spouse and children. One income supporting a family can be nearly impossible. If you have any form of debt or unhealthy spending habits, it can add unnecessary stress and frustration to the relationship. Debt and late payments tend to bring chaos and make peace of mind unobtainable. There is something liberating and stress reducing about being debt free. In my opinion, it allows your brain and body to work better because it is not bogged down by the stress that comes with debt. Address and adjust your spending habits before your spouse marries you and gets your debt too.

Debt is not the only issue that can cause arguments or divorce. If you want to not only get married but also stay married, I would consider the list that comes next and see if there are issues you can address as you get ready in this season.

Issues to consider:

- ✍ How you spend money
- ✍ How you use time
- ✍ How you honor and keep commitments
- ✍ How you prioritize your spouse and the relationship
- ✍ How you maintain relationships with family
- ✍ Infidelity
- ✍ Lying
- ✍ Unhealthy habits
- ✍ Respect in the relationship
- ✍ Communication
- ✍ Work ethic
- ✍ Drug use or dependency
- ✍ Stability
- ✍ Limitations
- ✍ Forgiveness and holding a grudge

There are more issues and topics than these but hopefully the list got you thinking. Consider areas that are already known weaknesses and consider coaching, mentorship or a form of accountability that best suits your needs. I listed areas that for me can be deal breakers.

One of my friends had a boyfriend and the relationship didn't last longer than a few months. He was cute, friendly, respectful, polite, and even took his hat off inside or at church. They were a cute couple until the cute wasn't enough. Unfortunately, their relationship was doomed from the beginning. From the beginning, to the middle and to the end, their issues were the same. She was working two jobs and he didn't have one. He was busy waiting for a big opportunity to come his way. The biggest problem with this is the waiting that was happening while he was playing video games and staying out late. He showed no interest in pursuing a job and I am almost certain that big opportunities don't come to people who are not already looking for them. Their work ethics and values did not match. Regardless of how hard she worked, he wasn't willing to find a job or start a career. He was looking for God to hand him something big to do and to this day, the big thing hasn't arrived.

Everyone is flawed. No one is perfect. Love and marriage are so much more than a wedding. It is looking past the imperfections to see the future that is made up between you and the one you cannot live without. It is recognizing and accepting every imperfection, every mistake, and every irritation and staying with them long after the I do has been said. I know that I am a hopeless romantic. I hope that in some way you add a little hopeless romanticism into your life and wait for the best thing in your life to arrive.

I have been told several times to make a list of what I am looking for in a relationship and in the man I want to marry. I used to say "God knows what I need and what I want and what I want is what

He has for me." I still believe this to be true, but I have also found comfort in making a list. The list is not long and some points are specific and non-negotiable while other things are connected to a heart's desire that I would love to be fulfilled but I will not be crushed if it doesn't happen. The benefit of making a list of what you are looking for is you will know it when you find it. Finding a spouse is not like going grocery shopping. You cannot go into a Men's Warehouse and leave with the man of your dreams, although if you try, will you let me know?

While you are waiting to get married, guard your heart.

When your friends get married before you do, you get to see what they do and figure out the best way for you. Not in a comparison but it's a free learning curve. You can learn from how they did it to see if you want it the same or different. For example, you can see wedding venues, understand the budget a modern wedding needs, the designer dresses or find out tips for the best honeymoon location. Learn what you like and what you don't like. It's okay to daydream, just don't spend your entire life there.

Before starting the next relationship, address the issues that brought the last one to an end. After I graduated high school the reasons for my parents' divorce became more and more of a reality. Though both parents made choices that led them to divorce, unfaithfulness was the ultimate cause for their relationship to end. From this, entering a relationship

> Before starting the next relationship, address the issues that brought the last one to an end.

started and ended based around my preconceived notion that every guy is a cheater. I would look at married couples and would think *he's a cheater*. Every guy was now guilty of cheating. This is not true and this was an issue I had to address in my head and in my heart before I could move on.

When people start dating they tend to start out as the ideal person they think the other one wants. In time, the relationship can end because the act of being something you're not is exhausting or you discover the real person you are dating and you don't like them. Be the real you from the beginning and stay you for always. Be comfortable and know that the person you just started dating doesn't deserve your heart right away. It's yours to give to the right person. A great friend once told me, "Girls mess up when they start dating a guy and wonder if this could be their husband. Girls should decide if the guy is a good boyfriend first and then wonder if they will make a good husband. No guy deserves to have your heart faster than that." From that moment on, this has been a guiding piece of advice that I willingly share. It is beneficial and scriptural to protect your heart.

> *Above all else, guard your heart, for everything you do flows from it.*
>
> Proverbs 4:23 NIV

While you're waiting to get married, keep your eyes open.

About a year ago, I decided I was going to start dressing a little nicer for the conferences and events where I was speaking. The reactions from some of my coworkers were pretty hilarious. One of them was convinced I had a secret boyfriend and I was dressing up for him. I was keeping my eyes open but I was also doing my best to make his eyes open if he was there and I didn't know it. I jokingly said, "The Bible says, 'He who finds a wife, finds a good thing.' So I am doing my best to make myself stand out." When I write "keep your eyes open" I mean it. Open your eyes to what God is doing around you, who He is bringing around you, and watch for His faithfulness to be proven.

> *He who finds a wife finds what is good and receives favor from the Lord.*
>
> Proverbs 18:22 NIV

I have kept my eyes open in every area of my life to see God move. I want to encourage you to do the same. Continue to believe God for His faithfulness. He will fulfill your heart's desire and you will see it happen in Jesus' name.

Questions for you to consider:

- How am I living faith with action?

- What compromise have I made in order to be in a relationship that is not good for me?

- When will I be willing to let go of relationships that are not beneficial for my life or my purpose?

- What areas of my life need to have more order or structure to prepare me for getting married?

- What character traits and habits have I found that I dislike from previous relationships?

ဢ What qualities am I looking for that I have
not found in previous relationships?

ဢ Am I willing to wait to be physically intimate
or wait to have sex until I am married?

ဢ Will I need accountability in order to
maintain my sexual purity?

ဢ Who can help me be accountable for
the decisions I am making?

My Prayer for You

This is my prayer for you while you are waiting to get married:

Heavenly Father,

I ask that as my friends read this prayer, you bring healing to their hearts. I pray that you surround them with comfort and restore their hope. Help them live their lives in the plan and purpose you have for them. I pray that you not only give my friends direction for the days ahead, but also open their eyes to see how wonderful lives are right now. I pray that you guard their hearts and I hope that they trust you with their hearts until you show them who to trust with it.

I pray for purity to be maintained in their hearts, minds and bodies. I pray that if their purity needs to be restored, that you would wipe away every memory from previous relationships. I ask that the desire to love and be loved would grow according to your plans and purpose for their lives. I ask that as my friends find (or get found by) love that you protect their love as they protect each other. Let the waiting time end quickly, in Jesus' name, amen.

Flee the evil desires of youth and pursue righteousness, faith, love and peace, along with those who call on the Lord out of a pure heart.

2 Timothy 2:22 NIV

My prayer for the one that will one day be mine:

I am waiting for you. I have had my moments of impatience and imperfections, but I have chosen to wait well for you. You already have my heart and I promise not to give my love to anyone but you. I have been praying for you and for our journey. I pray your journey is fulfilling and that you continue to pursue the passion inside of you. I am becoming the one you are waiting for. I pray you choose to wait well too and to steadily pursue all that God has for you every single day.

Epilogue: The Wife of Noble Character

A wife of noble character who can find?

She is worth far more than rubies.

Her husband has full confidence in her

and lacks nothing of value.

She brings him good, not harm,

all the days of her life.

She selects wool and flax

and works with eager hands.

She is like the merchant ships,

bringing her food from afar.

She gets up while it is still night;

she provides food for her family

and portions for her female servants.

She considers a field and buys it;

out of her earnings she plants a vineyard.

She sets about her work vigorously;

her arms are strong for her tasks.

She sees that her trading is profitable,

and her lamp does not go out at night.

In her hand she holds the distaff

and grasps the spindle with her fingers.

She opens her arms to the poor

and extends her hands to the needy.

When it snows, she has no fear for her household;

for all of them are clothed in scarlet.

She makes coverings for her bed;

she is clothed in fine linen and purple.

Her husband is respected at the city gate,

where he takes his seat among the elders of the land.

She makes linen garments and sells them,

and supplies the merchants with sashes.

She is clothed with strength and dignity;

she can laugh at the days to come.

She speaks with wisdom,

and faithful instruction is on her tongue.

She watches over the affairs of her household

and does not eat the bread of idleness.

Her children arise and call her blessed;

her husband also, and he praises her:

"Many women do noble things,

but you surpass them all."

Charm is deceptive, and beauty is fleeting;

but a woman who fears the Lord is to be praised.

Honor her for all that her hands have done,

and let her works bring her praise at the city gate.

Proverbs 31:10–31 NIV

Continue to believe God
for His faithfulness. He will
fulfill your heart's desire
and you will see it happen!

Chapter Five

While You Are Waiting

... to Have Children

One of my favorite things to pray over is couples who are trying to conceive but have been unsuccessful. I have witnessed all three of my sisters struggle with the desire to get pregnant and experienced delay to their pregnancy timelines. From natural conception to help with intervention from a doctor, I am thankful to see so many families become more complete with the addition of children.

While you are waiting to have children, have fun with each other.

I have seen it in movies and I have seen it in real life. When couples start to focus on getting pregnant and they adjust their love life to an ovulation schedule, the love and passion that they have for each other fades away. Every month of disappointment, every pregnancy test that shows a negative result, and with every hormone injection completed, love gets challenged and hearts can get hardened.

I remember being in a small town in Indiana. My mom was ministering at a few services and healing and miracles were happening. There were more than 200 people in the room and three women came specifically to get prayed for to have babies. They were married and each of them had been trying for a baby for as little as one year on up to three years. Each one of them reminded me of Hannah in the Bible, crying out for a baby and still unable to conceive. I prayed in the name of Jesus for each one of them and agreed with God for their lives and for the babies that their hearts' desired. At the end, the four of us were talking in a circle and I said, "Let me be blunt. Go back to having fun with your husbands. Don't think about trying to get pregnant or what the calendar says you should do. Be spontaneous and unplanned with him. Show him love just for the sake of loving him. Put on a feather boa if you have to, but do something to make the making love about the two of you again and not about making a baby."

A short time passed and our ministry team returned to a neighboring city in Indiana. All three of the women I had prayed with the last time were at the service too. I was looking forward to talking to them. Two of them were already pregnant! It had only been a couple of months. I was ecstatic, elated and overjoyed for two of them. My heart sank for the third friend who was not yet pregnant.

One of the most amazing miracles that I got to witness was the third woman's attitude. I could tell she was happy for the two women and it was genuine. She got to see God answer their prayers and respond to their hearts' cry. For me, it was hard not to be sad that she wasn't pregnant yet. I asked her how she was doing and there was a small ounce of sadness.

While you're waiting and believing God for anything there is always the possibility that you will see others receive it first. Do not get discouraged because someone else receives their miracle before you do. It is not a competition and it is not about how much God loves them or how much He loves you. How miracles happen is not something I can explain, but I can encourage you to wait for your miracle because it will be worth it.

> While you are waiting and believing God for anything there is always the possibility that you will see others receive it first.

While you are waiting, believe God and His promises for your life.

In Genesis, we see Abraham and Sarah long for a child. They go through struggle and strife, cross country moves, obey God, and still they were getting older and older. At one point, they had stopped trying to make it happen on their own, it was commonly known among their community that they were too old to have children. Even as God promised it would happen, there was still some time between the promise and the delivery. Abraham faithfully pursued the promise from God even when Sarah did not believe it could happen.

> *Then one of them said, "I will surely return to you about this time next year, and Sarah your wife will have a son." Now Sarah was listening at the entrance to the tent, which was behind him. Abraham and Sarah were already very old, and Sarah was past the age of childbearing. So Sarah laughed to herself as she thought, "After I am worn out and my lord is old, will I now have this pleasure?" Then the Lord said to Abraham, "Why did Sarah laugh and say, 'Will I really have a child, now that I am old?' Is anything too hard for the Lord? I will return to you at the appointed time next year, and Sarah will have a son."*

Genesis 18:10-14

Then, just as God promised, Abraham and Sarah had a son and named his Isaac.

> *Now the Lord was gracious to Sarah as he had said, and the Lord did for Sarah what he had promised. Sarah became pregnant and bore a son to Abraham in his old age, at the very time God had promised him. Abraham gave the name Isaac to the son Sarah bore him. When his son Isaac was eight days old, Abraham circumcised him, as God commanded him. Abraham was a hundred years old when his son Isaac was born to him. Sarah said, "God has brought me laughter, and everyone who hears about this will laugh with me." And she added, "Who would have said to Abraham that Sarah would nurse children? Yet I have borne him a son in his old age."*

Genesis 21:1-7

I love remembering Hannah crying out to God for a child. She loved her husband Elkanah and he loved her in return. In 1 Samuel 1, Elkanah demonstrates his love for Hannah and even tries to understand why she is so sad. He didn't understand or didn't see that Hannah was picked on and provoked for not having children. Back then wives, children and servants were signs of status. For Hannah, she wasn't able to have children so she could not add value to her husband's family. Finally, Hannah had a son and named him Samuel.

> Once when they had finished eating and drinking in Shiloh, Hannah stood up. Now Eli the priest was sitting on his chair by the doorpost of the Lord's house. In her deep anguish Hannah prayed to the Lord, weeping bitterly.
>
> And she made a vow, saying, "Lord Almighty, if you will only look on your servant's misery and remember me, and not forget your servant but give her a son, then I will give him to the Lord for all the days of his life, and no razor will ever be used on his head."
>
> As she kept on praying to the Lord, Eli observed her mouth. Hannah was praying in her heart, and her lips were moving but her voice was not heard.
>
> Eli thought she was drunk and said to her, "How long are you going to stay drunk? Put away your wine."
>
> "Not so, my lord," Hannah replied, "I am a woman who is deeply troubled. I have not been drinking wine or beer; I was pouring out my soul to the Lord. Do not take your servant for a wicked woman; I have been praying here out of my great anguish and grief."

Eli answered, "Go in peace, and may the God of Israel grant you what you have asked of him."

She said, "May your servant find favor in your eyes." Then she went her way and ate something, and her face was no longer downcast.

Early the next morning they arose and worshiped before the Lord and then went back to their home at Ramah. Elkanah made love to his wife Hannah, and the Lord remembered her.

So in the course of time Hannah became pregnant and gave birth to a son. She named him Samuel, saying, "Because I asked the Lord for him."

1 Samuel 1:9-20 NIV

When I pray for people to have babies, I pray and believe God, that just as He has done this for Hannah and Sarah, He can do it again. Hannah and Sarah were unable to have children despite the fact that their husbands were able to have children with other wives or servants. God can do the impossible, no matter the circumstances. Believe God for His promises for your life. Always believe, everything is possible.

While you are waiting to have children, be thankful for the babies that are coming to those around you.

There are not many moments in my life that I wish I could take back or undo. Allow me to share a moment that I wish I would have known how to handle differently. I remember being in Franklin,

Tennessee with my mom. I woke up to the noise of a text message that said, "We're pregnant." I looked at my phone and I was sad.

Babies are such a blessing. The more I find out about infertility, I am thankful when I find out people are pregnant. So why was I sad at this amazing announcement? The truth is, the text was from my sister who already had two children. I was sad, not because she had baby number three on the way, but because I was seeing another sister try to get pregnant for several years with no success. It was a bittersweet moment. I was excited for one and heartbroken for another. The moment I regret is found in the reply text message. I wrote back "you did it."

I can't imagine how much my lack of excitement and how hurtful my text message was to her. I have apologized and she has forgiven me but it was a moment and a message I would undo if I had the opportunity.

The other side of this story is this: the other sister (who had been trying to get pregnant for years) was already pregnant but had not told anyone. Previously, she had miscarried the day after telling everyone in the family she was pregnant and for fear of the same thing happening again, she and her husband were not telling anyone until she was twelve weeks pregnant. The pregnancy text message announcement came three days before the other sister wanted to share about her baby on the way. This created a little drama between the girls in our family, but thankfully all of it has been worked out. All of my nieces and nephews are happy, healthy, and growing up way too fast!

I hope that you can learn from my mistake. I hope that as you or someone you know goes through something similar, that you help them wait well and rejoice for the babies that are born among friends and family members. I know that a good attitude or the right response does not lessen the desire to have children, but do not allow your joy or happiness to be stolen because of how you feel in moments that will later define how well you waited.

While you are waiting to have children, hold onto hope.

My friends, Jason and Stephanie tried for five years to get pregnant. My mom prayed for them, in the name of Jesus, and within a few weeks they were pregnant. Nine months later, they had a healthy baby boy. Years had come and gone, the baby boy was growing up and they were ready for another baby. Their son turned 5, then 6, and then 7. As far as I knew, they were okay having one child. I only had that thought because I didn't know they had been trying for several years.

They resolved to go to a fertility doctor, get testing done and find out why they weren't getting pregnant. After working with the doctors and still no baby, the couple decided it would have to be God that would give them a baby. Their son is now ten years old and they have a baby girl. The doctors told the couple, without fertility treatments they had less than a 3% chance of getting pregnant on their own and because they did get pregnant and have a girl Stephanie said, "This baby is 100% miracle!"

After Stephanie got home from having the baby, I sent an email asking about the time they spent trying for a baby. I asked specifically, "While you were waiting for the baby—looking at the time period of trying to conceive and finally getting pregnant, what kept your hope up, gave you hope or inspired you to continue to trust God for a baby?" Here is her response:

"Jason and I both think what truly helped us is really knowing and understanding what the Word says, laying down our desires and really trusting Him. There were days that fear or doubt would sneak up on us but we constantly reminded ourselves that God is faithful and we wanted His will to be done in our lives. When we truly gave all control to Him we saw the miracle and plan of God at work. So many years we, and by we, I mean mostly me, took infertility in my own hands ... Seeing specialist after specialist. I knew what His Word said and when I took it literal and gave Him control I felt peace that I hadn't felt in years."

~Jason and Stephanie L.

They were able to step back and look at their relationship with God and be thankful for all that He had already done for them. From this position, they were able to believe Him for a baby, restore peace to their hearts and minds, and receive what their hearts' desired. Adeline is a miracle baby girl and an answer to so many prayers.

For one of my sisters, she and her husband were the image of perfect health and the right age. They were a perfect example for the best conditions for a natural conception. Time went on to prove something different. After visiting a specialist, it was confirmed. They were in the 20% of couples who had no explanation for not getting pregnant. There were no medical reasons, no physical cause or reproductive conditions that would prevent pregnancy. They just couldn't get pregnant.

For another sister, she and her husband decided to try to get pregnant and faster than you could spell "positive pregnancy test," they were pregnant. For their second child, they tried for more than a year to conceive before they were finally pregnant. They have four children and each one had a different journey and story behind how they got here.

For my youngest sister, through the help of a doctor, she and her husband were able to conceive. Their journey to becoming parents was filled with heartache, disappointments, shots and supplements and lots of waiting. After the baby was born, both parents relaxed into being a mommy and a daddy. The struggle to become parents was over. They could now love on their son that they had waited for, cried for, and hoped for. Their wait was finally over.

For my friends, Morgan and Jessica, they have a slightly different story for their three children. When I asked Jessica how they kept hope and faith in God for their family, here is what she said:

I was thinking of a good way to explain our story. The only way I know how to start is to go back to when the boys were about 5 and 7 years old, that's when we decided to try for another baby. I had not been on any type of birth control since Kaleb was 2 years old. My doctor put me on birth control for 6 months (to help regulate hormones) and said we could start trying after coming off it. Years passed by and still no baby.

I told Morgan I didn't want any kids in my thirties and I was getting closer and closer and then I was in my thirties. After a few years of being unsuccessful at getting pregnant, we started to become discouraged. It seemed that every month, somebody we knew was getting pregnant. We had people praying for us, and after numerous negative pregnancy tests, we decided that it was best we just be thankful for the two healthy boys we had, besides we knew people who couldn't even have one child.

Now keep in mind we hadn't been on any type of birth control in about 14 years. We kept telling ourselves,"If I suddenly became pregnant we'd be the happiest people, but if not, we were still happy with the life and family we had. In the back of my mind I knew that if God gave us a child this late, and mind you I'm not that old, but do have older children, without us ever having to do any special testing that there was a reason and a special purpose for Him choosing the timing.

November 2013, we decided that in the spring of 2014 I would have the procedure to remove the endometriosis and have the doctor tie my tubes during the process. But God had other plans because Alannah was conceived in January 2014. So I said all that to say yes, we did have hope. Hope that no matter if God decided it's a family of four and no more, His will for us was all we ever wanted.

~Morgan and Jessica W.

For Morgan and Jessica, they have children that are almost out of high school and now, a toddler. When I get to see them, I look at Alannah and I am so thankful for her sweet heart and cheerful disposition. She is a happy baby and she has brought so much joy to her brothers and to her parents.

In the process of writing this book, I reached out to several friends to get insight to a perspective that is different from my own. This next part is from friends who are still waiting and still trusting God to have children.

I have wanted a family and children my whole life. I never felt ready to take them on until recently. There are personal reasons for that. One is that I did not have a support system in place and would have essentially been on my own. Now I realize:

Nothing + God = Everything
... so I am not worried.

I had some severe health issues during my thirties. It was so severe that we were in survival mode, not family planning mode. I thought about children in my mid-thirties and although we were not trying we would have welcomed a child. I never got pregnant. Again, although I wanted children I was fearful that I was not ready and may not be able to handle it. I felt completely alone. Finally, when I gained a measure of healing we started to intentionally try to get pregnant. After many months of not getting pregnant I went to the doctor, did tests, and they showed that there was "nothing wrong". Went to more specialists - they could not see any reason that I could not get pregnant but it just wasn't happening. Time ticked on and on and I was still not pregnant.

We finally got insurance to help pay for IVF (In Vitro Fertilization) treatments and we were able to get some money to cover our share of expenses. Two IVF treatments availed nothing. The last one we paid for genetic testing of the embryo. It was missing 2 important chromosomes and would not attach or develop. I decided I didn't want to do anymore IVF treatments.

In the beginning I realize I was not in faith but fear. I was double minded. How could I expect anything? I was getting prayer but I was unsure I was ready - again, I was in fear, not faith. After the second IVF I actually gave up in my heart. I actually mourned never having biological children. The Lord has recently spoken some words to me and my faith is renewed to have children. Nothing is impossible for Him and I can do ALL things through Him, which strengthens me. I am not afraid anymore. We are doing our part and expecting a miracle!

~ Frank and Linda K.

While you are waiting to have children, be thankful for something different everyday.

For each of my sisters, I got to see their hopes and prayers for children get fulfilled. I have seen close friends lose a baby in the third trimester and seen friends bury their children after accidents or sicknesses caused their lives to end too soon. I have friends who are still trying with no rational reason to continue trying for a baby, but somehow God continues to give them hope in an almost hopeless situation.

Regardless of where you are in the process of making your family bigger, be thankful for something different everyday. One of the things that I am most thankful for is my oldest sister Charity and her husband Ted having children before I did. I started babysitting at such a young age; I started to see how I wanted to take care of my children. Seeing Ted and Charity have Luke and how they were raising him blew my mind. There were so many things that I didn't know. I am thankful for the example that I got to see while living with them and helping them with Luke and their other children for nearly six years.

When they had Kate, I was even more thankful to see how to they balanced marriage, working, a toddler and a newborn. Most people do not get this kind of hands on training.

My grandma and grandpa always said, "We always thought you would be the first one to get married and the first one to have children." My response was always, "Me too." When I heard this, I would respond in sadness. To me, it was a reminder that what I had believed God for still had not happened. I would shake my head or even lower my head in sorrow. Even though there was nothing that could be done to make me the first one married or the first one to have a baby, I felt like this was taken from me. The good news is I did not allow this to continue to effect my life or my happiness. Instead, I looked for the good side of this timing and how God could cause this to work out for my good and I believe He has so far.

This is where I am most thankful. The timeline I created for my life included getting married in my early twenties and having four children before I turned thirty. Now I think *what in the world was I thinking!?!* I can say my life would be entirely different had things gone according to my plan. I know that I would not have gotten involved in ministry, lived in Nashville or back in Houston, or even thought of writing a book. Most of the elements that have made my life as awesome as it is wouldn't have happened if my plan would have worked out. This is how and why I can be thankful for something different every single day.

I am in a position to speak into people's lives. I can pray for hope, healing, restoration or courage. This is all because I decided to make the most of life when it wasn't going according to my plan. I want to encourage you to do the same, be thankful for how things have turned out. When the baby finally comes or your heart is fulfilled through adoption, be thankful for everything around you.

Lord, the God of our fathers, Abraham, Isaac and Israel, keep these desires and thought in the hearts of your people forever, and keep their hearts loyal to you.

1 Chronicles 29:18 NIV

Take delight in the Lord, and he will give you the desires of your heart.

Psalm 37:4 NIV

Then God said, "Yes, but your wife Sarah will bear you a son, and you will call him Isaac.

I will establish my covenant with him as an everlasting covenant for his descendants after him. And as for Ishmael, I have heard you: I will surely bless him; I will make him fruitful and will greatly increase his numbers. He will be the father of twelve rulers, and I will make him into a great nation. But my covenant I will establish with Isaac, whom Sarah will bear to you by this time next year."

Genesis 17:19-21 NIV

May Prayer for You

This is my prayers for you while you are waiting to have children:

Heavenly Father,

I ask that you comfort my friends as they are reading this chapter. I pray that regardless of where they are in their lives, they would call on your name. I pray that you would heal their hearts from despair and disappointments. I ask for their tears of sorrow to become tears of joy. I pray that as they seek you—you will fulfill their hearts' desires. I pray and believe with them that they will have children!

In the name Jesus, anything that is preventing babies from being born or causing miscarriages, will be healed. I pray that anything that has been said by the doctors that would cause my friends to be hopeless, I command all of that to go in Jesus' name.

Any form of doubt, fear, or struggle in their mind, I command it to be gone in Jesus' name. Father, I ask that just as you gave to Abraham, a son within one year of your promise, I pray in your name and believe according to your word, for a healthy baby born at full term in within one year. Let the waiting time become the trimesters of life on the way, in Jesus' name, amen.

Questions to Consider

ᔕ   Make a list of things you love about your spouse.

ᔕ   Make a list of things you (probably) will not be able to do after you have children and make plans to do them.

ᔕ   What can you do or try to increase the passion between you and your spouse?

ᔕ   Are there things that you can change that would increase your chances of getting pregnant? (I.E. Supplements, weight loss, exercise, lower your stress levels, treatments, etc. It is important to remember I am not a doctor, but I have done research on this subject.)

ᔕ   Are there families around you that could use help with babysitting, childcare, grocery store runs, or home organization? (Something you can help with that will help reduce their stress.)

Be thankful for all God
has already done for you
while you wait for your
heart's desire.

Chapter Six

While
You Are
Waiting

... for Healing

Heal me, Lord, and I will be healed; save me and I will be saved, for you are the one I praise.

Jeremiah 17:14 NIV

Lord my God, I called to you for help, and you healed me.

Psalm 30:2 NIV

I remember suddenly waking up and it wasn't from the jetlag. I was in Ireland on a ministry trip and just as if someone had thrown a bucket of cold water on me, I was awake. Out of nowhere, excruciating pain was in my body. I had never experienced anything like this, but in an instant, I was very aware of my pain level.

I focused on my breathing. I tried to relax. I stretched. I curled up into a ball. Nothing could make me more comfortable or feel less pain. I prayed and I commanded the pain to go in Jesus' name. Nothing happened. I prayed again. I thanked God for my healing. Nothing happened. Minute after minute, I became a little more unsure of what was happening but I knew that God could heal me.

Nothing was happening. *Why wasn't I getting healed? Why wasn't the pain leaving?* I prayed again. I felt as if I were arguing with the devil or something. I knew God could heal me and I wanted it to happen. I wanted it to happen quickly. Nothing was happening. I felt horrible. Then I remembered that my mom was next door. I immediately said to myself, *"You do not need to go next door and wake her up so she can pray for you. You can pray on your own for your healing and God will heal you."* I closed my eyes and prayed again.

In my prayer I said to God, "I don't need anyone but YOU. You need to take this pain away because I believe that my prayer to you is just as effective as anyone else's. In the name of Jesus, I command this pain to go and for my body to be healed. Anything trying to attack it, I command it to go in Jesus' name." Within seconds my pain was completely gone. Within minutes I was asleep. My body came under the authority of Jesus Christ and anything that was trying to attack my body had left.

I want you to know the pain lasted not much more than thirty minutes and it is one of two instances that I remember as the most painful situations I have ever been through.

While you are waiting for healing, believe God and His word over your diagnosis or circumstances.

Jesus went throughout Galilee, teaching in their synagogues, proclaiming the good news of the kingdom, and healing every disease and sickness among the people. News about him spread all over Syria, and people brought to him all who were ill with various diseases, those suffering severe pain, the demon-possessed, those having seizures, and the paralyzed; and he healed them.

Matthew 4:23-24 NIV

I am thankful that my experiences with sickness have been as limited as they are. When I was a child, I had chronic sore throats that led the doctors and my parents to the decision to have my tonsils and adenoids removed. After the surgery, sore throats were a thing of the past and it was a solution that made my life better.

I truly believe God can restore health and heal the sick. God is a supernatural and mighty God. However, we live in the natural and need to obey natural laws. Taking care of the natural body is a lesson I am learning daily. I have not made the best choices and I have felt the consequences of not taking good enough care of myself.

From 2014 to early 2016, I have had several health issues regarding my reproductive organs. Everything has pretty much always worked like clock work until stress and complications from stress started effecting the way my body worked. In the fall of 2015,

I hit my limits on waiting for healing to happen without help from someone in the medical community. I was experiencing extreme fatigue, sleepless nights, difficulty waking up in the morning and high levels of irritation. In addition to these things, there were other physical issues that needed to be addressed. I wasn't myself. **I was tired of not feeling like me.**

I prayed and prayed for God to heal my body, but my body was not coming into agreement. I took supplements and sleep aids. I drank lots of water and avoided irritants as much as possible. One day, I gave up waiting for it to happen supernaturally. I felt completely broken. I couldn't keep going with the way that I was feeling. I had nothing left to help push me through.

I called my sister, who is a doctor in Arizona, and told her my symptoms. I explained what was going on and the time line of how long I had been experiencing the symptoms. From there, she was able to order blood work, and tested specifically to find the root cause of my issues. I waited longer than I should have to reach out for help. When I called her I was in the worst possible condition. I was beyond exhausted and could not battle chronic fatigue another day. Within a week of the bloodwork, the results came back and she was beyond concerned. Several of my blood levels were dangerously low. She recommended I immediately find a local doctor to start an infusion for the nutrients my body was lacking.

I made the appointment and met with the doctor. When I explained my issues to him, his response was, "The solution is most likely a hysterectomy." And with tears that came out of nowhere I said, "No. That is not an option or what I am willing to consider."

I was a new patient and already had my blood work that showed what I was lacking. He caught me off guard and his solution was not at all what I thought he would say. I did not expect his primary solution to be the death of my heart's desire.

I explained to him that he needed to help find a viable solution that would not prevent me from having children. Thankfully, he understood from that moment on that we needed to look in a different direction than surgery. As for my sister, she was able to look at my blood work to find a more realistic and less dramatic treatment.

I did not expect his solution to be the death of my heart's desire.

I thank God for my sister. She came up with a holistic treatment and it has brought healing to my body, mind, spirit and life. The treatment plan did not mask symptoms; it addressed the root causes affecting my health. It targeted the weaknesses in my body and made them stronger through supplements. My body has responded to the supplements and I am feeling like myself again. It's not completely perfect but I have had major improvements. There is more progress to be made, but it is happening daily. I am thankful that surgery was not the required option in order to find healing.

While I am waiting for my body to be completely healed, I am thanking God for every person I pray for who gets healed. I am thanking Him for healing me before and healing me again. I am praising God anyways and always just as I hope to encourage you to do the same.

Don't do what I did and ignore the small signs of sickness in your body. If something doesn't feel right or if you feel a little off, your body is trying to tell you something. For me, the first couple of doctors I went to didn't listen to my concerns. Their solutions were Band-Aids for the problems. I do not know where I would be today had I not listened to my body and finally made the call to my sister's office.

> *Spice,*
>
> *I am so thankful that you treated me like your patient and not just your sister. Thank you for your best possible care and concern.*
>
> *Thank you for your listening ears and your heart of compassion.*
>
> *Thank you for hearing me as I voiced my concerns and my fears.*
>
> *I love you and I am so proud of the doctor your have become and the medical practice you have built. I hope that just as you have been able to help me, that you are able to continue to help others find hope and healing for their lives.*

In all of the times where exhaustion tried to keep me down or pain tried to keep me from getting out of bed, I trusted and believed God for my healing. I prayed and believed for it and I never doubted that it would come. As I continue to get better, I will continue to believe God's word over my life, my health and my heart's desires. I will be completely healed and whole in Jesus' name.

Praise the Lord. Praise the Lord, my soul. I will praise the Lord all my life; I will sing praise to my God as long as I live. Do not put your trust in princes, in human beings, who cannot save. When their spirit departs, they return to the ground; on that very day their plans come to nothing.

Blessed are those whose help is the God of Jacob, whose hope is in the Lord their God. He is the Maker of heaven and earth, the sea, and everything in them—he remains faithful forever.

He upholds the cause of the oppressed and gives food to the hungry. The Lord sets prisoners free, the Lord gives sight to the blind, the Lord lifts up those who are bowed down, the Lord loves the righteous.

The Lord watches over the foreigner and sustains the fatherless and the widow, but he frustrates the ways of the wicked. The Lord reigns forever, your God, O Zion, for all generations. Praise the Lord.

Psalm 146:1-10 NIV

While you are waiting for healing, praise the Lord anyway.

My grandparents were always such an inspiration to me. I remember that my Grandma's response to any bad news or situation was "Well, praise the Lord anyway." This was truly an amazing thing to hear but to also learn. A response of praise the Lord anyway is powerful. It changes the focus from the situation, to the One who is able to change any situation.

Both of my maternal grandparents struggled with different sicknesses, as they got older. By the time they were in their eighties, they had both been in and out of medical rehabilitation facilities a number of times and their bodies were aging. With every trip to the hospital for a check up or for a midnight emergency room trip, they always praised the Lord. To them, they recognized this as an opportunity to lead a new doctor, technician, nurse or surgeon to the Lord.

For my grandparents, their health conditions created a salvation funnel. From the front door of the hospital, to the intake nurse, to the on call doctor, to the nurse assigned to their hospital room, they would tell them all about Jesus. They would never let anyone pass them by without telling them about Jesus and how much He loved them.

> Their health conditions created a salvation funnel.

My grandparents spearheaded efforts for door-to-door witnessing for the last decade of their life. Through their ministry and outreach around the world, they documented more than one million salvations. They lived and breathed the love of Jesus to everyone and they did this in spite of how they felt physically. They could have used any excuse to stop believing for healing, but they chose to praise the Lord at all times, through all things and in every way possible. In the end, my grandma passed away from congenital heart failure. She fell asleep here and opened her eyes in heaven. Less than a year from her passing, my grandpa, while listening to worship songs being sung around him, took his last breath on earth and passed peacefully into the arms of Jesus. I love the heritage that I have, the faith that they passed down from one generation to the next. It is exciting to meet people that tell me stories of how they met my grandparents and I enjoy hearing how their lives were impacted and improved because they met my grandparents.

While you are waiting for healing, pray, believe and thank God for healing those around you.

My grandparents were healing evangelists who paved the way for so many future ministries, authors and speakers. They taught people how to pray for the sick and see them recover. Some would say that it was "unfair" for people of such great faith to suffer with sickness before they passed away. I can understand what they mean, but I am so thankful that my grandparents didn't waiver in their relationship with God. They continued to believe and know that God is the healer. Even a few days before my grandma passed away she was praying for the sick and seeing them recover. She prayed for people on the phone while having to time her words with the oxygen that was being pumped into her nostrils. She praised the Lord always.

He sent out his word and healed them; he rescued them from the grave.

Psalm 107:20 NIV

Then Jesus said to the centurion, "Go! Let it be done just as you believed it would." And his servant was healed at that moment.

Matthew 8:13 NIV

While you are waiting for healing, thank God for how He has healed you before.

At the beginning of this chapter, I shared with you about the healing I received while I was in Ireland. It may sound crazy, but I realized afterwards how great a testimony this really was. It's an experience that I have, that I prayed and interceded for myself and got healed. My faith and trust in God grew out of this experience. Not only that, but I found a new level of determination. I wanted to experience a touch from God and I did. I know that on that day, I gained ground on a spiritual battlefield. I won a victory over my mind. I did not have to believe that someone else had to be with me to be healed. I experienced God taking all of the pain away and I will not doubt His ability to heal. This does not mean to avoid the doctor's office. If you need help, wisdom or treatment from a doctor, then take care of yourself and schedule an appointment.

Jesus is the provision for healing. He experienced the most humiliating beatings and death on a cross. He fought for us, to conquer the consequences of sin and death. He made a way so that we would spend eternity with God. It is through Jesus that we can experience an abundant life, receive healing, and the forgiveness of sins.

> But he was pierced for our transgressions, he was crushed for our iniquities; the punishment that brought us peace was on him, and by his wounds we are healed.
>
> Isaiah 53:5 NIV

You will again have compassion on us; you will tread our sins underfoot and hurl all our iniquities into the depths of the sea.

Micah 7:19 NIV

Then your light will break forth like the dawn, and your healing will quickly appear; then your righteousness will go before you, and the glory of the Lord will be your rear guard.

Isaiah 58:8 NIV

but the crowds learned about it and followed him. He welcomed them and spoke to them about the kingdom of God, and healed those who needed healing.

Luke 9:11 NIV

My Prayer For You

Heavenly Father,

I ask that you bring to remembrance any unconfessed sins, wounded feelings or disappointments not yet released to you. Anything that is blocking healing for my friends or causing a stronghold in their minds that would keep them from receiving their healing, I break it in Jesus' name, amen.

Take a moment and talk with God. Confess your sins or your shortcomings, give forgiveness where it is needed, and then pray again.

Consider This

- ℘ Praise the Lord at all times, through all things, in every possible way. Spend time and consider what conditions you were in before you needed healing?

- ℘ Are there circumstances or living environments that are adding to your stress level or sickness?

- ℘ What measures can you take to reduce these from affecting your health?

- ℘ Are there things you can do in the natural to eliminate pain or inflammation/causes for sickness?

- ℘ What changes to your diet or habits can be adjusted to increase your overall health?

- ℘ Have you researched and found a doctor who can help you feel better? ... get healthier?

Author's Note: <u>I am not a doctor.</u> The questions I shared above are those I asked and answered for myself. I have made changes to my life based on those answers. The changes have created a higher level of health in my body and life.

Chapter Seven

While *You Are* Waiting

... for Provision

O f all the things you or I could be required to wait for, I think one of the toughest ones to wait for is provision. There are two parts to consider while you are waiting for provision. The first is waiting, and the second is working while you are waiting. The two things must go hand in hand. Meaning: this will be the most active waiting period because while you are waiting, you should also be working. I have a lot of waiting and working experiences. I have found that my part was being responsible and working. God's part was honoring my efforts while I was waiting. I learned to trust God to have enough.

I have purchased three cars in my life only one of which was new. I learned it was okay and more than just okay to purchase a used car (thank you Dave Ramsey and Charity Bradshaw). During the year that I was at massage therapy school in Houston, I purchased a new car and by the time the third car payment was due, I was unable to come up with it.

I purchased the car and understood the monthly payment. I didn't get a crazy expensive car, but it became too expensive after my hours at work got cut nearly in half. I was working in retail and was doing really well in the company. I was making regular bonuses and worked close to forty hours every week. Suddenly, payroll hours for our location had to be cut back because the district wasn't doing well overall. I went from working 38-40 hours a week to 20-24 hours a week. Some weeks were better but it was inconsistent.

Time came for the next car payment and I was coming up short. I was barely able to pay the third payment and it was nearly two weeks late. Now the fourth payment was due and my paycheck was not able to cover it. I was worried and started thinking *what did I get myself into?*

I was almost finished in the intern program for massage therapy. I was driving from my mom's house back to my grandparents' ministry when out of nowhere a guy in a huge Bronco ran a red light and plowed over the front end of my car. After he hit me, he hit two other cars. I was in the middle of the intersection when the accident occurred. From the way his truck hit my car, it tore the hood from one side to the other and then pushed it through the front window.

That day my brand new car was completely totaled. It had 2,400 miles on it and the force at which he hit my car was so strong that it broke the frame. I was in shock but extremely thankful to be alive. He hit the front end of my car and destroyed any possibility of it being safe to drive again. I walked away with only a scratch from glass cutting my finger while I was getting out of the car.

Within three months, the accident was settled. His insurance company paid off the balance of the car, gave me a small personal settlement, and then gave me the matching amount of what was put down on the car when I bought it.

Even though the accident scared me, this is a perfect example of how God can cause things to turn around for our good. The accident helped me learn to trust God and not in my circumstances. After the settlement, I bought a used car and had a car payment that was one third less than what it was with the new car. The horrible accident is now a testimony of God's protection and provision for my life. The ability to pay my car payment was restored because I was able to afford this car even on a smaller paycheck.

While you are waiting for provision, be faithful with your tithe.

Most people consider the tithe to be a financial gift based on 10% of their annual income. For me, a tithe is simply this, 10% of all my increase. So what do I mean by "all my increase"? I mean 10% of my paychecks, birthday money, Christmas money, or honorariums. I also tithe on what comes into my business. I want every aspect of what comes to me to be blessed. I know that giving 10% is a minimum, and I like living in the blessings of obedience.

Giving is one of my favorite things to do. I love giving gifts or giving of my time, talent, or resources as God leads me to give. When I am unable to give and help meet the needs around me, I pray and ask God to trust me with more so I can give more away. I trust and believe God to honor His word and I have seen His faithfulness over and over again.

> *"Will a mere mortal rob God? Yet you rob me. 'But you ask, "How are we robbing you?"'*
>
> *"In tithes and offerings. You are under a curse—your whole nation—because you are robbing me.*
>
> *"Bring the whole tithe into the storehouse, that there may be food in my house. Test me in this," says the Lord Almighty, "and see if I will not throw open the floodgates of heaven and pour out so much blessing that there will not be room enough to store it.*
>
> *"I will prevent pests from devouring your crops, and the vines in your fields will not drop their fruit before it is ripe," says the Lord Almighty.*
>
> *"Then all the nations will call you blessed, for yours will be a delightful land," says the Lord Almighty.*
>
> Malachi 3:8-10 NIV

If you haven't tithed before, or if it has been awhile since you tithed, understand how closely obedience to God's Word is linked with your provision.

While you are waiting for provision, listen and give as God speaks to you to give.

I remember sitting in church and the time came for the tithes and offerings to be received. I heard God speak to my heart to give 20% from what I had made that week and what I was going to make the next week doing massage therapy. I felt my heart stop for a quick second. TWENTY PERCENT? I felt I was doing really well staying faithful with my 10% and trusting God to help me keep my bills paid in full and on time. He said again, "Give twenty percent from what you made this week and from what you will make next week." I got out a piece of paper and added up what the two weeks should look like. I wrote out a check for 20% and put it in the offering as the bucket passed by.

I sat there for a minute with the thought of *what did I just do and I hope everything works out.* The following week, all of my appointments went well. I made what I thought I would make and was thankful that none of my clients cancelled.

The amazing part, and truly God gets the glory for this, is one of the clients that I was working for had a group of people that would be coming in town for a big event and he wanted everyone who wanted a massage to be able to get one. This was huge! I negotiated a great rate for the day and in that one day I made more than the 20% I had given. Not only did the booking show how God honors His word, but also that same week I was given a digital camera, a memory card and a case for the camera. The camera came with a note that said, "Because you don't have one and I thought you would like it."

I was completely blown away by the day of work I booked and the camera on top of it! I completely believe that when we trust God with our finances and are faithful in the tithe and offerings, that He will rebuke the devourer for our sake.

If you fully obey the Lord your God and carefully follow all his commands I give you today, the Lord your God will set you high above all the nations on earth.

All these blessings will come on you and accompany you if you obey the Lord your God: You will be blessed in the city and blessed in the country.

The fruit of your womb will be blessed, and the crops of your land and the young of your livestock—the calves of your herds and the lambs of your flocks.

Your basket and your kneading trough will be blessed. You will be blessed when you come in and blessed when you go out.

The Lord will grant that the enemies who rise up against you will be defeated before you. They will come at you from one direction but flee from you in seven.

The Lord will send a blessing on your barns and on everything you put your hand to. The Lord your God will bless you in the land he is giving you. The Lord will establish you as his holy people, as he promised you on oath, if you keep the commands of the Lord your God and walk in obedience to him. Then all the peoples on earth will see that you are called by the name of the Lord, and they will fear you.

The Lord will grant you abundant prosperity—in the fruit of your womb, the young of your livestock and the crops of your ground—in the land he swore to your ancestors to give you. The Lord will open the heavens, the storehouse of his bounty, to send rain on your land in season and to bless all the work of your hands.

You will lend to many nations but will borrow from none. The Lord will make you the head, not the tail. If you pay attention to the commands of the Lord your God that I give you this day and carefully follow them, you will always be at the top, never at the bottom.

Do not turn aside from any of the commands I give you today, to the right or to the left, following other gods and serving them.

Deuteronomy 28:1-14 NIV

While I was working in retail, I learned a lot about people and how complicated lives can get when marriages do not work out and what happens where there are children involved. I became friends with one of my co-workers even though she and I didn't always see eye to eye. I like to think that she helped me grow up in areas that were my shortcomings and I know from her words that "through our friendship" she rededicated her life to God.

One night my friend called me scared that her electricity was going to be shut off because she was behind on paying the bill. From there her worries escalated because if the power was out her ex-husband could get custody of their children. Her stress level was the highest I had ever seen it. I came up with a solution. I offered her my credit card to put the electric bill on and then said she would not have to pay me back. She immediately said no. She wouldn't take my credit card number because she was worried that it would be too much for me to handle.

I told her I could take care of it and that I believed that God would supply for me just as I was able to supply for her. I said, "If He doesn't, then it is still something I can afford to do and it will all work out." I fully believed that God was going to bless this and that He would find a way to get this money back to me.

About a week later, my mom asked me to give two of her friends a massage. I wasn't going to charge my mom for this work and I honored her by giving my talent (in the form of massages) to her friends. When the massages were over, the two people said thank you and then one of them gave me a tip with a twenty-dollar bill on the outside. I said thank you in return and put the money in my pocket. After that, my mom wanted to show them where her office was and take them to lunch. I got invited to go with them and on the way I shared with them about my friend's electric bill. I shared how I believed God to send provision back to me.

Everyone in the car enjoyed the story and had something similar to share. It was such a great afternoon and I loved getting to know my mom's friends. While we were at mom's office, I went into the other room to take care of a couple of things. I ended up reaching into my pocket to get the keys and when I got the keys out the money fell out and landed on the floor. I reached down and picked it up and before putting it in my pocket I unfolded the money to see how much it was. It was $250! It was the exact amount of money that the electric bill was. I went back to my mom and to her friends and said, "This is it! I knew God was going to supply for this!" and then I told them the amount of the electric bill and I couldn't believe how God would supply the provision needed so quickly. The electric bill was paid off before the end of the billing cycle!

You will be enriched in every way so that you can be generous on every occasion, and through us your generosity will result in thanksgiving to God.

2 Corinthians 9:11 NIV

One year for Christmas I was given a really beautiful thank you letter. Inside the letter I was hoping to find a fun, little Christmas check but there wasn't one. I looked again to read the letter. The letter expressed gratitude and deep appreciation for how I had been helping the author of the letter. They went on to write that they wanted to give me up to $2500 toward paying off my car. The only catch was it was a matching gift. The letter went on to say that any amount, from the minimum car payment up to $2500 over the next two months, they would match dollar for dollar.

At the time I owed roughly $5700 on my car. I looked at this as an incentive as well as a challenge. I decided to work as much as I possibly could and live on as little as possible for two months. I was doing massage therapy at the time, but I also sent out emails and text messages letting people know I was available to house sit, pet sit, babysit, car pool, or anything else to earn income. At the end of the two months I was able to pay off $5000! My arms hurt from my hands working so hard but I can tell you this, it was worth it.

Another great detail to this experience is I chose not to limit where or what I did for work. In trying to find odd jobs I explained that I had this major opportunity and whatever I was able to pay off on my car someone else was matching it. At the end of the two months, there had been several

I chose not to limit where or what I did for work.

occasions where people had written me checks or given me cash knowing it would be doubled.

There will be opportunities that present themselves to you. They can be doors that lead to future jobs, relationships, connections or even more opportunities. How you handle an opportunity or an open door will determine the options and provision that comes from the next open door. **Remember to consider that the opportunity requiring work could be the answer to prayer that was said while waiting for provision.**

> *But remember the Lord your God, for it is he who gives you the ability to produce wealth, and so confirms his covenant, which he swore to your ancestors, as it is today.*
>
> Deuteronomy 8:18 NIV

I have shared a few examples in which working for provision was the key to creating it. What I want to share with you now is how God created the supply and how it had nothing to do with work I did or could ever do. There are more examples than what I will include in this book but I tell you the truth, I have never gone without and I will never doubt God's faithfulness to provide. I know that financial generosity comes from people. I have been blessed because people have listened to God and gone out of their way to be obedient.

Provision does not always mean money. There are many things that you and I could need that money cannot buy like joy, friendship, self-worth, peace, trust, healing, direction, wisdom, respect, and purpose. These are only a few but it's a good start.

While you're waiting for provision, wait with your eyes open.

I was helping my mom with a ministry service in Midland, Texas. She was praying for people and they were getting healed. One lady came up and wanted her eyesight restored. My mom prayed and nothing happened. She wasn't blind, but her eyesight had gotten weaker and she wanted to be able to see without her glasses. My mom prayed again, and again nothing happened, at least, not to the lady.

A boy sitting in the service shouted out, "WHOA!" and everyone turned to look at him. He said, "I was just sitting here looking at my shoe laces and then where I was looking it was blurry, but then it got all clear. I don't even know what happened."

He wasn't paying attention to the service or anything that was happening in the room and God moved in that room and healed the boy's eyesight. It was in an instant and his eyesight was perfect.

This is the moment that I got a little irritated. I know that sounds terrible but it is true. I had been praying for months and months and maybe even longer for God to heal my eyesight. I did not mind wearing contacts but I believed God could restore my eyesight so that I would not have to wear them anymore. So I thought to myself *God, why did you heal his eyes when he is not even paying attention? He wasn't even asking you for it and you did it anyways.*

I know now that God used that moment to get the boy's attention. He demonstrated His awesome power and love for the boy even though the boy was showing no interest in what was happening that night.

Have you ever had a moment like this? I know that I have had moments where I have been totally oblivious to what God was doing around me and then He demonstrated His love for me.

While you are waiting, you may not see how provision is on its way.

Healing and miracles can happen at any moment. What is even more amazing is when God makes them happen and you don't see them coming. After the service in Midland **Healing and miracles can happen at any moment.** I continued to travel and help my mom with her ministry. I'm not sure of the exact amount of time that passed after Midland, but I do know that enough time had passed that I stopped waiting and believing for my eyes to be healed.

I was in Phoenix, Arizona and attending a conference with my mom. She was sitting a row in front of me and she turned around and our conversation went about like this:

Mom: "If you could get Lasik done on your eyes, would you get it done?"

Me: "Do you know how much that costs? It is crazy expensive. I'm not spending that kind of money on my eyes."

Mom: "That's not my question. My question was 'If you could get Lasik done on your eyes would you get it done?'"

Me: "Yes" and I smiled.

Mom: "There is a doctor I know that does Lasik and offers a 'Friends and Family' discount. I am going to ask how much it is after the discount and see if this is something I could do for you."

I smiled at the thought of getting Lasik done but I didn't focus on the possibility. In my mind I was thinking a discount could be given and the price could still be insanely too much. Instead of getting my hopes up and then getting devastated that it couldn't happen, I left the idea there in the category of a wonderful possibility.

About a month after that I got a call from my mom and the doctor had offered to do Lasik on me as well as two of my sisters for an extremely discounted, jaw dropping, super tiny fee. I nearly fell over! The cost was so minimal I was in shock. In that moment, I quickly asked, "Can you find out how much it would be for Tiffany (my best friend) to get Lasik done too?" I figured if the doctor was willing to give us such an amazing offer why not ask if one more could be included.

Shortly after that, my mom forwarded an email from the doctor that said God had spoken to him to perform the Lasik on my sisters and me for free! I kept reading and the doctor included giving Lasik to Tiffany and two friends of our family! There were a total of six of us that were given Lasik, none of which could have earned it or paid for it. It was a supernatural blessing into all of our lives and a beautiful answer to prayer for provision that God honored.

For the six of us, none of us saw this miracle while it was on its way. Each of us had a different experience that led us to receiving this special gift. For me, I got tired of waiting and believing God to heal my eyes. I got impatient and pretty much accepted the fact that I would have to wear contacts for the rest of my life. I know that God used this as a way to get my attention and to speak life into my faith in Him. I knew and still know that He is the healer but what I learned from this is He doesn't always do it in a way that we see it coming.

God is creative in His generosity and how He displays His love for us. He has done it before and He can do it again. He might do it differently—He might surprise you with the way He works.

While you are waiting for provision, trust God to honor His word.

I know and believe that God is more than able to meet my needs. I know that He is more than able to provide for you too. When I was in my early twenties, my pastor was sharing a message when he spoke something that has stuck with me for more than fifteen years. He said, "When you're believing God for something, thank Him for what He has done for others, thank Him for what He has already done for you and thank Him for what you know He will do for you again."

When I pray and believe God to honor His word, I look at what He has already done for others and I know that if He can do it for them, He can do it for me. I look into the Bible to see the miracles that have happened and believe that if they could have happened back then, they can happen right now.

The Widow's Olive Oil

The wife of a man from the company of the prophets cried out to Elisha, "Your servant my husband is dead, and you know that he revered the Lord. But now his creditor is coming to take my two boys as his slaves."

Elisha replied to her, "How can I help you? Tell me, what do you have in your house?"

"Your servant has nothing there at all," she said, "except a small jar of olive oil."

Elisha said, "Go around and ask all your neighbors for empty jars. Don't ask for just a few. Then go inside and shut the door behind you and your sons. Pour oil into all the jars, and as each is filled, put it to one side."

She left him and shut the door behind her and her sons. They brought the jars to her and she kept pouring. When all the jars were full, she said to her son, "Bring me another one."

But he replied, "There is not a jar left."

Then the oil stopped flowing. She went and told the man of God, and he said, "Go, sell the oil and pay your debts. You and your sons can live on what is left."

2 Kings 4:1-7 NIV

God supplied provision beyond what the widow had room to contain. She was told by the prophet Elisha to go and borrow vases and every single vase was filled. The oil did not stop flowing until she ran out of containers. God not only supplied enough for the debt to be paid if full, but He supplied even more so that the family could live on the extra. This is supernatural provision and I hope it encourages you to create a space to receive and contain the provision that is coming. Fill your waiting room with expectation of delivery and supernatural supply.

God can pour on the blessings in astonishing ways so that you're ready for anything and everything, more than just ready to do what needs to be done. As one psalmist puts it, He throws caution to the winds, giving to the needy in reckless abandon.

His right-living, right-giving ways never run out, never wear out. This most generous God who gives seed to the farmer that becomes bread for your meals is more than extravagant with you.

He gives you something you can then give away, which grows into full-formed lives, robust in God, wealthy in every way, so that you can be generous in every way, producing with us great praise to God.

2 Corinthians 9:10 MSG

For God is the one who provides seed for the farmer and then bread to eat. In the same way, he will provide and increase your resources and then produce a great harvest of generosity in you.

2 Corinthians 9:10 NLT

Now may He who supplies seed to the sower, and bread for food, supply and multiply the seed you have sown and increase the fruits of your righteousness,

2 Corinthians 9:10 NKJV

My Prayer for You

This is my prayer for you as you wait for God to supply your provision:

Dear Heavenly Father,

I ask and I pray that you would bring peace to the minds of my friends. I pray that as they put their trust in You, You will make a way where there seems to be no way. I ask that overtime, bonuses, withheld pay, or blessings out of the blue would make their way to my friends. I ask that as they are faithful with what they have, that You will fill in the gaps and provide provision. I ask for creative ideas, strength to work more hours, favor at their places of employment and for the companies they work for to be blessed by You. I ask that you would lower their stress levels and that the constant worry would be removed. I ask all of these things in Jesus' name, amen.

Things to Consider

- Name several ways you could create provision.

- What could you be doing to help manage the provision that you have now?

- Write down three things you could stop buying (even for a little while) to help produce provision with your own ability.

ဆ Take inventory of the things that surround you and describe how God is moving around you.

ဆ Describe how God has brought provision into your life in the past.

ဆ Combine faith with action then create a place for the provision you need.

Chapter Eight

While You Are Waiting

... for Promotion

It may seem obvious to say make the right choice, but when you have no options that feel right or do not care for any of your options, what do you do then? Consider your options and make the best choice. I have discovered several keys to making the best choice when the right choice was hard to find. A few keys would be: pray first, then apply wisdom. From there, seek Godly counsel or advice from leaders who live by example. I have endured learning curves that could have been avoided had I considered Godly counsel and prayer before making significant decisions.

While you are waiting, consider your options and make the best choice.

I remember graduating with my trade school degree and completing the internship. Our class was one of the best that the owner of the school had seen and he made a point to tell our class that two positions would be made available to graduating interns. Graduating and starting my career with a job offer would be ideal. Once I heard about the two positions, I started to pray for direction and to hear God about this job opportunity. I was confident that my work was just as good, if not better, than most of my classmates. It wasn't arrogance; I was basing this on my reviews and the feedback from my instructors. As everyone completed the internship, and the final student turned in her notes, the job offers were made public. I was not one of the two students invited to work at the school.

In the same moment that my feelings were hurt because I knew my work should have been recognized, I also found comfort in knowing God was directing my steps. It was more than just a job opportunity at hand. I found this trade school while I was going through one of the toughest times in my life. After my plans for college changed because of my parents' divorce, my mom moved to the Houston area to help my grandparents with their ministry. I was an adult, but could not afford to live on my own and stay in Dallas.

The rational decision was to move to Houston and stay with my mom. Even to this day, when I think about whether or not I should have moved to Houston, I can remember that it wasn't something that I prayed about. I didn't look to God for direction. In the short time that I lived in Houston, I questioned where God was and what

He was doing. How could a loving God allow me to feel so lost, alone, abandoned, depressed? I made the decision to move without talking to God about it and once I was there I blamed God for leaving me there all by myself.

Six months or so after moving to Houston, I remember talking to my youth pastor. One of the best things that I got from our conversation was the insight to my situation. I moved myself away from my home church and friends and moved to the "wilderness." He asked me, "Melody, did God even tell you to move or did you move because you couldn't find another option?" From this, I started praying more about where my life was. I asked God to give me greater direction for my life.

At the time of graduation, I had been in Houston for just short of a year. As graduation got closer and closer, my prayer became more about where should I live and enjoy life versus should I stay in Houston where I was struggling to be happy and to find friends. Through prayer and probably a childish mindset, in my final prayer about what to do after graduation I said, "God, if I am supposed to stay in Houston I will get one of the two job offers. If I don't, then I'm moving back to Dallas."

Within two weeks of graduating from trade school, I drove to Dallas and looked for an apartment. My church was going to be what I rebuilt my life around. The relationships and leadership at the church were a huge source of strength and encouragement in my life. I knew that proximity was key to reestablishing who I was and who I was going to be. I remember sitting and looking across the lake that is close to the church and prayed and asked God about my new location. This is where I wanted to be, but I wanted Him to bless this decision.

There have been several moments in my life that I can look at and recognize how the Holy Spirit guided me. I can see now the challenging circumstances and situations that were meant to hurt or distract me from my calling, were navigated by the Holy Spirit. It is just as if I am riding down a river seeing the situation but not being affected by it.

While you are waiting, learn how to work well with others.

Sometime ago, I got into a situation where I wasn't able to get along with someone near me. There were several attempts to resolve the situation and restore the relationship, but each effort only ended in a dead end. As time progressed, things gradually got more difficult and I was getting overwhelmed with stress to the point of having a couple of panic attacks. The craziest part is the entire situation should have never made it as far as it did. I was left feeling out of control, afraid, taken advantage of, and really hurt. It's important to know that I wasn't perfect or flawless in this situation, but I did strive to forgive and be forgiven.

Unfortunately, things didn't head for restoration. At this point, I felt completely helpless. Everything that I had tried, failed. I prayed and asked God to take control of the situation, but nothing was showing improvement. All of the joy and love of what I was doing was taken away from me. I hated where I was and knew that something had to change.

In every situation, the only thing that you can have control over is yourself. I looked at this situation and said, "I can only work on me." But what could I do? At this moment of clarity, I went into the closest bookstore in search of personal development books. I remembered that my pastors in Nashville used John C. Maxwell books for mentorship and leadership team development. Right then, I scanned through all of his books on the shelf and found the one titled *21 Indispensable Qualities of a Leader*. I purchased it after reading the back of the book. This was just what I needed! Within the first few chapters, I realized how much I needed the wisdom this little book with a big title contained. I started with a hopeless situation and realized that the solution to the problem was this: I needed to work on me. Reading about the qualities of a leader gave me clarity, insight, and direction for the hopeless situation. Amazingly enough, I grew as a person and as a leader and the once hopeless situation resolved itself.

I needed to work on me.

A huge light bulb went off in my head and in my heart. While I was reading about the qualities of a leader, I found information on The John Maxwell Team. I love teaching and speaking; their training offers development and certification in these areas. I knew the next thing I needed to do was to invest in my ability as a speaker. Finding this training and development was the good that came out of the bad, just as God promises.

And we know that in all things God works for the good of those who love him, who have been called according to his purpose.

Romans 8:28 NIV

I live and breathe this scripture every single day. I often encourage people to look at their situation or circumstances and ask God to show them the good. I have found that when you look to find the good in all situations, you can find it.

There are several scriptures and Biblical recordings of God giving direction. He gently guides us to live in the plan and purpose that He has for us. There are circumstances that arise, hearts that get broken, and lives that end too soon. God is faithful and will honor His word. Just as David would sing of a loving God, it is good to remember and focus on who God is and what He does.

A Psalm of David

The Lord is my shepherd, I lack nothing. He makes me lie down in green pastures, he leads me beside quiet waters, he refreshes my soul. He guides me along the right paths for his name's sake.

Even though I walk through the darkest valley, I will fear no evil, for you are with me; your rod and your staff, they comfort me. You prepare a table before me in the presence of my enemies.

You anoint my head with oil; my cup overflows. Surely your goodness and love will follow me all the days of my life, and I will dwell in the house of the Lord forever.

Psalm 23:1-6 NIV

In Exodus, we see how God uses Moses to deliver the Israelites out of Egypt, into the wilderness and finally into the promise land. Specifically, we see how God guides the path out of Egypt.

When Pharaoh let the people go, God did not lead them on the road through the Philistine country, though that was shorter.

For God said, "If they face war, they might change their minds and return to Egypt."

So God led the people around by the desert road toward the Red Sea. The Israelites went up out of Egypt ready for battle. By day the Lord went ahead of them in a pillar of cloud to guide them on their way and by night in a pillar of fire to give them light, so that they could travel by day or night.

Neither the pillar of cloud by day nor the pillar of fire by night left its place in front of the people.

Exodus 13:17-18 and 24 NIV

Moses listened to the voice of God. He listened to the directions given to him by God and left what was familiar to him. He led the Israelites out of slavery. We know the story doesn't end there, but I do want you to see how your obedience to God can do the same thing for those around you. It's in the wilderness that the Israelites needed to learn how to hear God and to follow His commandments.

While you are waiting, understand that God establishes promotion.

In Daniel 3, we see how King Nebuchadnezzar used his power to rule over and force the kingdom to worship gods that are not the one true God. King Nebuchadnezzar created a golden idol and he commanded everyone to stop what they were doing and worship it.

Loud music played throughout the kingdom and that was their sign to stop and worship the golden idol. When the king commanded that everyone worship the idol, he also made a bold punishment for those who did not obey. Three young Jewish men who loved God refused to worship the idol. The men knew that would be thrown into a fiery furnace if they did not bow down and worship the idol.

Shadrach, Meshach and Abednego replied to him, "King Nebuchadnezzar, we do not need to defend ourselves before you in this matter. If we are thrown into the blazing furnace, the God we serve is able to deliver us from it, and he will deliver us from Your Majesty's hand. But even if he does not, we want you to know, Your Majesty, that we will not serve your gods or worship the image of gold you have set up."

Daniel 3:16-18 NIV

The three men were thrown into the fiery furnace and flames were so hot that the guards who threw them in were killed immediately. The king saw that there was a fourth man walking in the furnace with Shadrach, Meshach and Abednego. It was God that protected the men and even walked in the fire with them.

Then Nebuchadnezzar said, "Praise be to the God of Shadrach, Meshach and Abednego, who has sent his angel and rescued his servants! They trusted in him and defied the king's command and were willing to give up their lives rather than serve or worship any god except their own God.

Daniel 3:28 NIV

Do not change who you are or what you believe in order to achieve promotion. Honor and respect yourself as you show that same honor and respect to others.

How to Make Yourself Promotable

As you pursue promotion, consider adding additional efforts in the following areas. In my opinion, if you use these keys, you can unlock doors to promotion. It may not come from the company you are currently with; you may find that other companies will take interest in you. Your promotion may come from the doors opening at a new company.

First Key:

Give the company you work for the best version of yourself. Your dress code should reflect the position you want not the position you already have. This may be as simple as wearing dress pants or slacks instead of jeans. This may include wearing a nicer pair of shoes instead of wearing tennis shoes. This could also mean that your hair style needs to be updated or more maintained.

Second Key:

Give your all and do not hold anything back. In my opinion, most people who work on a set salary will work their required hours and go home. That is fine for them, but that is not fine for you. If you work in a salaried position, make it your goal to be the first one there and the last one to leave. This will not always be required. If you are looking for promotion, you will have to do something to make yourself stand out above the crowd. The crowd doesn't go above and beyond, but you do. Find out what the expectations are for the current position you are in and then find a way to go beyond expectations. Stay consistent with your efforts. Managers do not like inconsistency in the work place.

Third Key:

Take time management courses. If you can find a way to become more productive in less time you will stand out among your coworkers. If you can develop an accurate plan for your team to accomplish more, increase the profit margin and reduce absenteeism, you will make yourself more valuable to the company. Bring increase where you are to create opportunities where you want to go.

Fourth Key:

Improve communication skills. Learn how to communicate with coworkers, as well as, upper and lower members of management. If your company is looking for bilingual employees, then consider learning a new language. Learning an additional language increases your value to the company.

Fifth Key:

Build your skill set. Gain a better understanding of software programs and help those around you develop their skill set. If you can help your coworkers better understand programs that they need in order to have a better performance review, you are adding value to your department as well as to your company.

Sixth Key:

Be the solution to the problem. If you know of a problem that your company has, then you can search and find the solution. Most employees know of ways to improve the company they work for, unfortunately, they do not know how to implement them. If you can become the solution to the problem, you have one more area to demonstrate your value, worth and expertise to your company.

Seventh Key:

Be a leader. Do not worry about your title. Be willing to be the leader that influences without a title. To use this key most effectively, I would highly recommend one of my favorite books: *The 5 Levels of Leadership: Proven Steps to Maximize Your Potential* by John C. Maxwell.

Eighth Key:

Be resilient. When you get knocked down, get back up. Les Brown, top motivational speaker is known for saying, *"When life knocks you down, try to land on your back. Because if you can look up, you can get up. Let your reason get you back up."* If you have been passed over for promotion, set an appointment with your manager and find out what they think is holding you back.

> **"The greatest glory in living lies not in never falling, but in rising every time we fall."**
> —Nelson Mandela

My Prayer for You

This is my prayer for you while you are waiting for promotion:

Heavenly Father,

I pray that promotion is coming quickly, that the waiting time is coming to an end. I thank you that my friends are working diligently to honor You and produce good work in their current position. I thank you for the preparation time that my friends have had and that the right door of opportunity is going to present itself quickly. I thank you that my friends have studied to show themselves approved by their coworkers, managers and those who create the opportunity for promotion. I thank You for anointing their hands and multiplying their efforts as they glorify You in all they do, in Jesus' name, amen.

Things to Consider

∞ God gives you the power to create wealth.

But remember the Lord your God, for it is he who gives you the ability to produce wealth, and so confirms his covenant, which he swore to your ancestors, as it is today.

Deuteronomy 8:18 NIV

∞ Humility is part of the path to promotion.

∞ Don't be anxious, trust God.

∞ Stay alert—What are you doing to develop yourself?

∞ How can you use your abilities to bring greater profitability to your company (or organization)?

∞ Do you work well with others? Are you teachable in your current position?

∞ Ask God to make you strong, firm, and steadfast.

Humble yourselves, therefore, under God's mighty hand, that he may lift you up in due time.

Cast all your anxiety on him because he cares for you.

Be alert and of sober mind. Your enemy the devil prowls around like a roaring lion looking for someone to devour.

Resist him, standing firm in the faith, because you know that the family of believers throughout the world is undergoing the same kind of sufferings.

And the God of all grace, who called you to his eternal glory in Christ, after you have suffered a little while, will himself restore you and make you strong, firm and steadfast.

To him be the power for ever and ever. Amen.

1 Peter 5:6-11 NIV

If you look for the good
in every situation, you
will find it!

Chapter Nine

While You Are Waiting

... for Grief to Go

I am thankful for so many different things in my life. When I think of my family and for the grief that I have experience with, I am thankful that I have not had to endure the heartache or pain that I have seen others experience. It's more than the loss that caused grief, it can be difficult to find joy in the after effect of loss.

When there is a sudden loss of a family member or close friend, the emotional trauma is immediate. There is no way to plan for it, prepare your heart for it, or have the opportunity to resolve conflict. When sickness comes and latches onto a person, then takes every hope for healing away, there is usually a timeline or an estimation of life expectancy. Having more notice does not stop the sting of death. It does not make the grief easier to understand or adjust to.

The only benefit is the possibility to resolve conflict and restore relationships.

While you are waiting for the grief to go, acknowledge your emotions.

When I was a teenager, my Granddad passed away while mowing the lawn. He lived a long and full life. I remember my dad telling my sisters and me that he died and he died while doing something that he loved. I didn't process this information as fast as my sister Spice did. She immediately started crying and asked about Granny. Then she got really upset because she had written a letter to Granny and Granddad and they had not received it yet. It was mailed the day before Granddad died. She begged my dad to find the letter and stop it from being delivered. Spice was very concerned with Granny getting the letter because it was addressed to both of them. My dad assured Spice that Granny would still love the letter and that she would not be hurt or upset about it being addressed to both of them.

Our family went to his funeral and went on to the graveside. I remember crying and getting a little upset but I know that I was more upset for my family then for my Granddad dying. At the graveside, I remember almost getting angry just before we left. My Granny, a feisty little lady, went over to where Granddad was buried and started pulling flowers out of the arrangements. As she grabbed a few more flowers she said, "Everyone, grab some flowers. He doesn't need them anymore." I was in shock. I couldn't believe she was pulling flowers to take home with her. Thankfully, this was happening while only our immediate family was there. I did not understand why this made me more upset. I know now it was the lack of respect shown to him the disturbed me.

July 14, 2009, I was with my mom in Denver, Colorado. Her phone rang and she woke up to the news that her mom, Frances Hunter, had passed away during the night. I remember getting upset and crying because at that moment one of my greatest heart's desires had become impossible. My prayer and hope was for my grandparents to meet the man I would marry, and at that moment I realized it would never happen.

My Grandma had been sick for several years. It wasn't a huge shock that she was gone. There was peace in knowing that she was completely pain free and enjoying her new freedom and mobility in heaven. For me, the grief was easier to heal from because I knew she was better off.

I never allowed myself to get upset again, to become emotional or to grieve for the loss of her in my life. About a year after she passed away, I got hit really hard with emotions that I didn't allow myself to express at the memorial service or anytime sooner. I started crying and for a few seconds I completely let go. Then I shook my head side to side and told myself, *"It's been too long now. Shake it off and stop it."* I made myself stop crying because I told myself, *"At this point, it's been too long so accept it and move on."* It was in those few moments that I denied the feelings of grief and loss to be felt. I know that ignoring it did damage to my heart and it is something that I would do differently if ever given the opportunity.

Since her passing, I have had several dreams of seeing my Grandma, of talking to her, and was even able to hug her and kiss her. The dreams were a gift from God. They are not the same as seeing her again, but it is closure and healing for my heart. The last dream I had that I got to see her, I ran to her and kissed her on the cheek and said, "I'm going to do this while I can." It was only moments later that I woke up because of the tears in my eyes. I was happy because the dream felt so real.

While you are waiting for the grief to go, prepare yourself and make arrangements.

My grandma was sick for several years before she passed away. There were several close calls and even a couple of occasions when the entire family went to see her in the hospital. One instance in particular comes to mind when we caravaned two full car loads from Houston to Dallas, only to arrive in Dallas to get a phone call from her doctor, letting us know she most likely would not make it through the night.

We loaded up both cars and drove right back to Houston. We arrived very late at night and we were able to get into the hospital to see her. As we stood around her bed, with all of the monitors and tubes connected to her, we told her how much we loved her and how much she meant to each of us. That night she had a miraculous recovery and lived for more than two years after that trip to the emergency room.

Sometime later, when she was feeling better and was back at her office, I went to see her. I told her I had a horrible question for her and I needed her to understand my heart. That day I asked her to write a letter to the man I would marry. I explained my concerns over the possibility for her to be in heaven before I could get married. I went on to say that I wanted him to have something from her and grandpa, something that was just for him. Later that day, she dictated the letter into a tape recorder and her secretary typed it and placed it in a pink envelope. Grandma and grandpa signed and sealed the letter then addressed it to: *The Husband of Melody*. This precious letter has been in a safety deposit box since then and it will continue to wait there until it is needed.

Asking my grandma for this letter was not an easy conversation but I am so thankful that she understood my love for them and how significant they are to me. I believe that because I had this letter and had considered the possibility of her passing before the timing of meeting my husband helped me through the grief of losing her when I did.

I was recently at a conference and one of the key note speakers owns a funeral home. I was surprised that she spoke on preparing now for what will come later. I never considered planning ahead beyond knowing I wanted to be buried and not cremated. She explained in such a short period of time that most families and friends argue over the details of the service and burial. As she spoke, she encouraged people to write out what they want for their funeral or memorial service. At first, I thought this sounded crazy and morbid, but then I realized how it truly makes sense.

> Prepare now for what will come later.

She recommended writing it out from what music you want played or songs you want sung, to the outfit you want to wear, colors and types of flowers you prefer, who would say the opening prayer, the preacher, the pallbearers, and where you would like to be buried or if you would like your ashes spread. I know this sounds crazy. She gave several examples of family members at each others throats over decisions. I cannot imagine arguing over the details for the funeral of a family member so I added this information into the book. By letting people know exactly what you want, you will help them through the planning and grieving of your passing.

While you are waiting for the grief to go, feel it for yourself.

Grief affects people differently. "While many will relay common grieving experiences, every grieving experience is unique, as it's in relationship to different relationships lost. If you or someone you know has lost someone you know that grief may be something that doesn't completely go away, but instead evolves and weaves into your life, lessening during some hours and making its presence known during others. No one can truly predict how long grief will last, but we do know one thing, it is a natural and important process in remembering and feeling the connection to those who have passed. The intensity of the grief informs us how deeply we can feel for ourselves and for others. It informs us of the deep love we have in our hearts."[1]

I asked a friend to share a little of her grief process in the aftermath of loosing her daughter at such a young age.

From my friend Lori:

A parent's worst nightmare is outliving their child. You don't expect it, you don't welcome it, and you sure don't embrace it when it happens. That is exactly what happened to me. I woke up the morning of February 17, 2013, and never expected my day to end in a nightmare.

Now, looking back, I see God's fingerprints all over every detail—starting with bringing her home that night before. My daughter was supposed to spend the night at a friend's house, but God brought her home to me before He brought her home to Him. I am grateful for those moments with her—we laughed, we had lunch together, and we hugged and said "I love you" before we both left home in separate cars. It was those precious moments with her, those precious words she spoke to me that are sealed in my heart. He gave them to me as a treasure to hold on to. That was closure, and I realize a gift that not every person receives.

You see, my daughter was my life and my everything. I was a single mom for 16 years, and my sole purpose was to raise my daughter. I worked to support her, to give her a home, to put her through school. When I wasn't working, we were at school activities, sports events, or doing homework. I was her constant, and she was mine. Then, one choice changed it all. In one instance, she was taken from me. In one moment, my joy turned to sorrow, and my dancing stopped.

In one choice, our family went from one of happiness to one of grief. In my opinion, grief is one of the heaviest and most painful emotions that a human heart can experience. It is complete brokenness from the inside out; it affects our mind, body and spirit. No one can escape it; grief will affect each one of us at some point in our life. I have never felt loss so destructive before, and life became void and *meaningless. My very reason for living was no longer with me. I had no purpose, no direction, and no desire to live.*

Within a couple of months after her death, I started attending a support group called GriefShare. My life was so out of control—I couldn't focus on anything—my every thought was about her and the loss; I was numb except for the ball of burning pain in my chest. GriefShare taught me that I wasn't going crazy or losing my mind, but everything I was experiencing was a part of the grieving process. I would rather know what exactly was happening to me, and not just walking blindly. I learned several important keys during this journey:

1) Grief affects each person differently. No one grieves the exact same way.

2) Grief is based on love. How deeply you love is how deeply you can grieve.

3) Grief is not healed overnight.

4) God is the only one who can heal grief, and He does it with His Love. Love is the only thing that can truly heal grief.

Yes, I believe grief can be healed. While I was walking through grief, I had many people tell me "oh, you will always grieve for her" or "you just have to learn to live with the pain" or "you will never get over the loss." Those platitudes always put a check inside my heart, and I chose not to believe them. I am an ordained minister, and I have served under a healing evangelist for over ten years. In those ten years, I've seen multiple miracles performed— physically and emotionally. One truth in that foundation is this—God heals all— all people, all sickness, all disease, all emotions.

> *And Jesus went about all Galilee, teaching in their synagogues, and preaching the gospel of the kingdom, and healing __all__ manner of sickness and __all__ manner of disease among the people. And his fame went throughout all Syria: and they brought unto him __all__ sick people that were taken with divers diseases and torments, and those which were possessed with devils, and those which were lunatic, and those that had the palsy; and he healed them."*
>
> Matthew 4:23 – 24 KJV

When God says all, He means all physical sickness, all emotional sickness; all means all, exclusive of none. The only factor in this is you have to allow Him access to your heart to bring healing and wholeness to you again. If you shut down, close your heart and build walls, it delays healing and hardens your heart. A hard truth is you have to face and feel the pain in order for Him to heal your heart. If you believe those platitudes, then you are saying that grief is bigger than God, and that is just not true.

Being a believer does not give you a free pass to not grieve. We just grieve differently from unbelievers.

> *" And now, dear brothers and sisters, we want you to know what will happen to the believers who have died, so you will not grieve like people who have no hope."*
>
> 1 Thessalonians 4:13 NLT

God tells us we grieve with hope. Hope is powerful. Hope was the only cord that I clung to in my grief journey. I know my daughter is in heaven with Jesus, and my hope is one day to see her again.

My Prayer for You

This is my prayer for you while you are waiting for your grief to go:

Heavenly Father,

I ask that you comfort my friends as they grieve the loss of someone or something that they really loved. I ask that you bring to mind good experiences, funny stories, inside jokes, and little moments that mean so much.

I pray that they will not get trapped by the heaviness of grief, but that they will move through the waves of it with Your help and strength. I pray that this chapter has brought encouragement and direction for navigating through grief. More than anything, I ask that my friends will not feel alone anymore. I pray that they will know that you are with them always, in Jesus' name, amen.

Things to Consider

℘ Grief is a process, not an event. Give yourself permission to grieve and be patient with the healing process.

℘ Invite God into your grief. Let Him feel it with you and allow His Holy Spirit to comfort you. Your tears matter to Him. He bore your sorrows.

ဆာ Take care of yourself while you grieve. Be sure not to neglect your health and your need for rest. Be sure to do things that replenish you.

ဆာ Grief is not forever. If you find yourself stuck in chronic sadness, unable to deal with loss, seek help from someone who can walk you through inner healing. Restoration is meant for you!

Endnote

1.   Elisha Goldstein, Ph.D. Retrieved from: http://blogs.psychcentral.com/ mindfulness/2009/02/feeling-grief-means-being-alive-7-tips-to-help.

The foundation is this:
God heals all—
all people,
all sickness,
all disease,
all emotions.

All means all.

Chapter Ten

While
You Are
Waiting

You Can Become
Significant

In order to do or be anything of significance, you will need to make time to connect with people around you. I say "make time" because you will have to make it available. It will be your choice and how you decide to spend or invest your time will make all the difference.

If you hired a contractor to build a house, gave him access to the land and money to pour the foundation but six months had passed and no progress had been made on your house, would you continue to give the contractor more money to inspire him to start building? I certainly hope not. Investing your time into people is like giving money to the contractor. You only have a certain amount of time to invest, so you will want to make sure your time and availability is honored and respected by those you in which you are investing.

Whether you are investing in family, friends, or work, it is more than time management. It must be a personal commitment and it must be intentional.

One of the best things or phrases I have learned was said by my friend, Wendy K. Walters. She was speaking at a conference and said, *"In order to accomplish your goal, some areas of your life may require intentional neglect."* This blew my mind! Intentional neglect is like saying "not right now" to commitments, obligations, or activities that could require more time than what you have available.

In the middle of writing this book, I had to step away from it for a few weeks. The obligations and responsibilities for where I work was higher than the priority of completing a chapter or hitting a word count. Then, in order to complete this book and publish it on time, hanging out with family, friends or even playing with my dog, had to be a lower priority temporarily. I had to intentionally neglect the desires to go to the movies, attend concerts or travel, in order to accomplish the final pages of this book. To me, intentional neglect is a temporary shift in obligations or priorities in order to produce a desired outcome. If you want different results, you will have to intentionally do something different.

> **"Insanity: doing the same thing over and over again and expecting different results."**
> **—Albert Einstein**

"You have it within your power to make your life a great story, one of significance. Every person can. Regardless of nationality, opportunity, ethnicity, or capacity, each of us can live a life of significance. We can do things that matter and that can make the world a better place. I hope you believe that."

—John C. Maxwell, *Intentional Living*

I have learned how to add value to those around me from attending conferences and reading books by John C. Maxwell. I enjoy listening to him teach and share his passion for adding value to others. I learned from him to do everything with excellence and to go beyond simply meeting expectations. He inspires me to develop my dreams of speaking and writing and how I can make a difference.

I hope to do the same for you. You can make your life what you want. If you are tired of where you are, then do something different today. Make a different choice, take a different path, or step in the direction of your dreams. You only have so many breaths to breathe and so many days to live. I do not want you to look back with regret. I want you to look forward with anticipation and look back with excitement over your accomplishments.

You can make your life what you want.

When you decide to live life with the intentions to enjoy every moment and make the most of every opportunity, you will find that you are also adding the most value to those closest to you. Invest your knowledge, wisdom and experience, in people around you to make the greatest impact on the generations to come.

> ## "It isn't your visibility, but your contribution that matters."
>
> —**Wendy K. Walters**, *Intentionality: Live on Purpose!*

How You Can Become Significant

"Do you know the difference between success and significance? I know a lot of people who believe they are successful because they have everything they want. They have added value to themselves. But I believe significance comes when you add value to others— and you can't have true success without significance."[1]

Step One to Significance:

Be teachable. If you already know it all and you are unwilling to learn something new, you will be unable to grow as a person, a leader, or an influencer. If you are willing to learn and more importantly, be taught, it will be recognizable to those around you. People who have gone before you or who have advanced beyond where you are currently, will notice your teachable attitude and they will share with you what they have learned and how they learned it.

Successful people are always looking for the next generation of leaders and business owners. They do not want to die with the knowledge they have acquired still inside them. They look for protégé's. Being teachable will make you available for significance.

Step Two to Significance:

Be approachable. If people are uncomfortable talking to you or being around you, it will be nearly impossible for you to add value to them. A rude attitude or a "I can't be bothered" attitude will prevent you from working well with your coworkers or team and it will lead to an inability to be significant in your life and the lives of those around you. If people have questions and you have the answers, but they are uncomfortable when talking to you, do what you can to make yourself more approachable.

Try being more available for coffee or lunch appointments. Make things less formal to help reduce the stress felt by those around you. Be willing to serve those around you. Serving will open up the lines of communication and it will change people's perspectives of who you are to them. Being approachable will make you available for significance.

Step Three to Significance:

Be authentic. Be who you really are all the time. In my opinion, our society is tired of watching people pretend that they have it all together. People are in search of genuine and authentic people to connect with. There may be days or situations that you will need to carry yourself like you have it all figured out, but if you continue to fake it until you make it, you will end up a really good actor instead of you who really want to be. Being authentic will make you available for significance.

Step Four to Significance:

Be proactive on your priorities. Plan your day and plan for your priorities. If you have one hundred things that need to get done today, start with the most important thing and place it at the top of your list. Aim to complete the list in an order that would give you the greatest return on your time invested in them. Start with the greatest return on investment and then gradually cross the items off your list.

> Being proactive with your priorities will make you available for significance.

Larger projects or more time consuming projects may not have the best advantage for you or your day. Organize and identify your priorities so you can understand the value of your time and the value of your team. When you are proactive on achieving your priorities, a sense of accomplishment will come to you and you will achieve more than you thought you could. Being proactive with your priorities will make you available for significance.

Step Five to Significance:

Be intentional for personal growth. Sixty seconds make a minute, sixty minutes make an hour and twenty-four hours make a day. This will always be the way time works. Everyone only gets so much time; can you make a difference with yours? Eight hours are spoken for by the company you work for (more if you are the owner). Around eight hours a night is committed to sleeping or trying to sleep. What do you do with the remaining hours of every day? Possibly you have commuting to work, taking children to and from school, going to church services, going grocery shopping, cooking meals, doing laundry and cleaning your home. Where can you put intentional growth into your day?

At the end of the day, how can you be intentional for personal growth? Plan your day, prioritize your time, then set an appointment for your personal growth. When you are getting ready in the morning or while you are driving, listen to teachings, podcasts, or messages that will share elements for personal growth. When you are winding down at night, read books that explain elements of personal growth that interest you.

When you plan your year, set aside time to attend an event or conference that will help you develop your personal growth. Being intentional for your personal growth will make you available for significance.

My Prayer for You

This is my prayer for you as you become significant while you wait:

Heavenly Father,

I pray for my friends as the idea of personal growth or development might be new to them. I pray that you give them wisdom and knowledge as they desire for more of those things. I pray that you will guide them on their journey to greater personal development.

I ask that you connect them with the right people and bring new relationships to them in order to create growth in their walk with You and to their personal development as well. I also ask that as they develop, they will look for ways to add value to people around them, that they would look to help others as well as themselves. I ask all of this in Jesus' name, amen.

Questions to Consider:

∞ Do I have a plan in place to nurture my personal growth and development?

∞ Do I control my priorities, or do the priorities of others control me?

∞ Am I the starring role in my own life?

∞ Am I approachable? Do others feel like I am easy to access and communicate with?

∞ Do I actively seek to learn new things, process new information, and stretch myself—am I teachable?

Endnote

1.   John C. Maxwell. Retreived from: http://www.success.com/article/john-maxwell-success-or-significance. August 31, 2010.

Chapter Eleven

While You Are Waiting

Place Your Life Before God

Place Your Life Before God

So here's what I want you to do, God helping you: Take your everyday, ordinary life—your sleeping, eating, going-to-work, and walking-around life—and place it before God as an offering. Embracing what God does for you is the best thing you can do for him.

Don't become so well-adjusted to your culture that you fit into it without even thinking. Instead, fix your attention on God. You'll be changed from the inside out. Readily recognize what he wants from you, and quickly respond to it. Unlike the culture around you, always dragging you down to its level of immaturity, God brings the best out of you, develops well-formed maturity in you.

I'm speaking to you out of deep gratitude for all that God has given me, and especially as I have responsibilities in relation to you. Living then, as every one of you does, in pure grace, it's important that you not misinterpret yourselves as people who are bringing this goodness to God. No, God brings it all to you. The only accurate way to understand ourselves is by what God is and by what he does for us, not by what we are and what we do for him.

In this way we are like the various parts of a human body. Each part gets its meaning from the body as a whole, not the other way around. The body we're talking about is Christ's body of chosen people. Each of us finds our meaning and function as a part of his body. But as a chopped-off finger or cut-off toe we wouldn't amount to much, would we? So since we find ourselves fashioned into all these excellently formed and marvelously functioning parts in Christ's body, let's just go ahead and be what we were made to be, without enviously or pridefully comparing ourselves with each other, or trying to be something we aren't.

If you preach, just preach God's Message, nothing else; if you help, just help, don't take over; if you teach, stick to your teaching; if you give encouraging guidance, be careful that you don't get bossy; if you're put in charge, don't manipulate; if you're called to give aid to people in distress, keep your eyes open and be quick to respond; if you work with the disadvantaged, don't let yourself get irritated with them or depressed by them. Keep a smile on your face.

Love from the center of who you are; don't fake it. Run for dear life from evil; hold on for dear life to good. Be good friends who love deeply; practice playing second fiddle.

Don't burn out; keep yourselves fueled and aflame. Be alert servants of the Master, cheerfully expectant. Don't quit in hard times; pray all the harder. Help needy Christians; be inventive in hospitality.

Bless your enemies; no cursing under your breath. Laugh with your happy friends when they're happy; share tears when they're down. Get along with each other; don't be stuck-up. Make friends with nobodies; don't be the great somebody.

Don't hit back; discover beauty in everyone. If you've got it in you, get along with everybody. Don't insist on getting even; that's not for you to do. "I'll do the judging," says God. "I'll take care of it."

Our Scriptures tell us that if we see our enemy hungry, go buy that person lunch, or if he's thirsty, get him a drink. Your generosity will surprise him with goodness. Don't let evil get the best of you; get the best of evil by doing good.

Romans 12:1-21 MSG

Embracing what God
does for you is the
best thing you can
do for Him.

Chapter Twelve

While You Are Waiting

It's Your Life: Live It and Love It

I am a firm believer that if you go for what you want and persevere, you can achieve your dreams and get what you want. It will happen. **Everything is possible!** I was speaking at a conference in Chicago and at the end of the service I had the opportunity to speak one-on-one with a few of the attendees.

When I looked at one lady, I noticed she appeared to have it all together. She was dressed nicely and had her hair done. She kept it all together until I looked in her eyes. In her eyes, I could see that she was desperate and hurting. God spoke to my heart and I shared it with her. This is what was said: "You need to try again. You can do it. You almost made it happen. You almost got what you wanted but then the resistance stopped you. Resistance can only last so long, so you just have to last longer than it. It will happen if you try again. When you try again, you'll need help from a couple of key people. They will help support your dream and encourage you to persevere. Resistance will come again, but this time you will be strong enough to beat it. So will you try again?"

If you will outlast resistance, you will get what you want.

It's YOUR life. You can make it what you want it to be. Will you allow people or circumstances to stand in the way of what you want or what you want to accomplish? If so, you will fill your life with wishes and regrets. **The fear of regret should scare you into an active role in your life.** You cannot control those who are around you, but you can control if you let them stand in your way.

You can live your dreams.

Dreams are not meant to torture you for what you cannot have, they are meant to inspire you to reach beyond that for which you have settled. They are there to encourage you to go for more of what you love in life.

"Go confidently in the direction of your dreams! Live the life you've imagined."

—Henry David Thoreau

You can do it.

Taking the first step in the direction of your dream could be the hardest or the slowest. The first step is necessary to create momentum. Momentum will help you move faster and with ease. Don't stop moving in the direction of your dreams.

> **"In the end, it's not the years in your life that count. It's the life in your years."**
>
> **—Abraham Lincoln**

You can have what you want.

I love the movie *Forrest Gump*. I know he is a fictional character but the movie is inspiring on so many different levels. Forrest is a friend who loves and cares for everyone; he doesn't understand prejudice or hatred, he only knows how to love and care for those around him. I love how Forrest always looked after Jenny, took care of her and waited for her to come home every time she left. At times, it bothered me that he waited so patiently and faithfully. This movie was so popular that it is still referenced by t-shirts and catch phrases. Just recently I discovered that I disagree with one of the most popular quotes from this movie:

> **"Life is like a box of chocolates. You never know what you're going to get."**
>
> **—Forrest Gump**

I believe that you can have what you want when you take time to order it that way. Yes, there are variables and circumstances that will arise and they will make you create a back up plan. **Your entire life should not be a back up plan for what you really want.** It is my opinion, life is like a box of chocolates and you can order the flavors you love the most! I discovered this idea after a trip to See's Candies, a store at the mall. They are filled with different types of chocolates, candies, and sweets. You can select the size of the box you want and then select the candy that you want put in it. **You can order it the way you want it.** Life can be the same way. By now you have discovered what you like and what you do not like, what you want more of and what you would like less of; start to order your life to be the way you like it.

You only get one chance to make life what you want. Even while you are waiting, regardless of what you are waiting for, today is your only day to do something with, so make it a good one.

"You only live once, but if you do it right, once is enough."
—Mae West

You can be happy.

Life may have given you lemons. May I suggest you set up a fruit stand and make some money from it?

On my journey to make the most of my life, I have received inspiration from my relationship with God, courage from what I have seen others go through, and boldness to pursue my dreams from my inner circle of friends. I have always had passion, but every once in a while, it is good to rekindle the passion for what you love.

I desire to help you find self-worth for the pursuit of your dreams. No one else can accomplish what you are here on this earth to accomplish. You could be the solution that people are looking for right now. Regardless of what you are waiting for, look at your life and make the most of it. Take inventory of all of the things that make you happy and fulfilled, then start doing more of those things.

No one else can accomplish what you are here on this earth to accomplish.

If you are having a hard time coming up with things to be happy about while you are waiting, here is a short list of things that make me happy.

Swinging on a swing

Sitting on the porch

Minions

Road trips

Slurpees®

Spontaneous dancing

Singing along to a song in the store

Flip flop weather

Thunderstorms

Paid time off

Eye contact with a stranger

Sailing

Burt's Bees lip moisturizer

Deer eating grass

Snuggling

Live music

Painting pottery

Sleeping in

Sunsets

Holding a baby turtle

FaceTime

Free wifi

Playing cards

Free upgrades

Holding the door for a stranger

Waving

Getting an 18 wheeler to honk

Walking on soft grass

Warm towels

Seeing Blue Bonnets on the side of the road

Taking pictures

Reading a good book

Baby chicks

Crying over good news

Successful potty training

Goldfish

A great playlist

Cable

Cows walking in a pasture
Sign language
Take out
Netflix
Bubble tea
Guacamole
Fireworks
Seeing dolphins in the ocean
The end of the construction zone
A great hair day
Gift cards
Car washes
Puppies
Tickets to the game
Green lights in a row

Use my list and then make your own.

While you are waiting, you can be happy and make the most of every single day. At the end of the day, every day, I hope you have gotten closer to catching the dreams you chase. It is your life. Be happy. Be fulfilled. Be you.

"You have brains in your head. You have feet in your shoes. You can steer yourself any direction you choose."

—Dr. Seuss

My Prayer for You

This is my prayer for you as you learn to live and love your life!

Dear Heavenly Father,

I pray that as my friends step out to enjoy their lives, you will keep them strong and make them brave. Let them find new and amazing joys in life. Let them discover who they are meant to be and how to live their lives and love them.

More than anything, I pray that this book has shown them how to make the most of where they are in life. I pray that the time spent in the waiting room has been an investment into who they are becoming each and every day. I ask that they find happiness and fulfillment every day, in Jesus' name, amen.

"While you are in life's waiting room remember this: You only get one opportunity to LIVE your LIFE and LOVE IT!"

—Melody Barker

Appendix

Meet Melody Barker

Melody Barker is a coach who knows how to make people promotable! With wisdom beyond her years, Melody captivates audiences. She leads willing participants down the path of how to accomplish their mission, how to discover and map out their unfulfilled plan, and how to reach for the fulfillment of purpose God has for their life. She will show you how to LIVE your life and LOVE it!

A John Maxwell Team Certified speaker and coach, Melody has a passion for leadership development and reaching personal potential. Her focused pursuit of this passion is evident in every presentation and coaching opportunity.

If you are looking for life changing inspiration that sparks change and reveals insight for overcoming obstacles, Melody Barker is your next divine appointment!

Attitude is Adjustable. Purpose is Powerful.
Everything is Possible.

- ✇ **Invite Melody to Speak**

- ✇ **Sign Up for Leadership & Personal**
  Growth Training Events

- ✇ **Engage Melody as Coach ... Get Promotable!**

w w w . m e l o d y b a r k e r . c o m